C000019516

THE CHURCH OF THE LIVING GOD

Ulf Ekman

Word of Life Publications

THE CHURCH OF THE LIVING GOD
First published in English, 1994

ISBN 91 7866 283 4
ISBN 1 884017 10 X USA

Printed in Sweden for Word of Life Publications by ScandBook AB

Word of Life Publications
GPO Box 2375, Brisbane, Qld 4001, Australia
Box 641, Marine Parade, Singapore 9144
Box 17, S-751 03 Uppsala, Sweden
Box 70, Oxted, Surrey, RH8 0YS, United Kingdom
Box 46108, Minneapolis, MN 55446, USA

Acknowledgments
Unless otherwise indicated, Scripture quotations are from the
Holy Bible, New International Version, copyright © 1973, 1978,
1984 International Bible Society. Used by permission of
Zondervan Bible Publishers

Other Scripture quotations are from the *New King James
Version* of the Bible (NKJV), copyright © 1979, 1980, 1982
Thomas Nelson, Inc; *King James Version* (KJV)

Contents

Preface

The Church is God's unique creation in this Age of Grace. It was a hidden mystery, until Jesus' resurrection from the dead and the outpouring of the Holy Spirit at Pentecost. Sadly, the concept of the Church is still a mystery to many today. God is doing mighty things through the lives of individual believers and He wants to multiply this through the Church, collectively. Therefore, I am convinced that the Lord wants to give you a clear revelation and understanding of His Church. This is not a peripheral issue; it is central. Church members can know God's will and His calling. They can learn what His power can do for men and women.

In the Last Days, the Church will be tested and tried as never before, but it will also become all that God has planned. The End-time Revival that will sweep through the earth, will have both its source and climax in the Church. God wants you to understand this, so that you can find your place and be actively involved in a strong, growing local church. I believe this book will give you that understanding.

Ulf Ekman

1

The Foundation of the Church —The Vision

I also say to you that you are Peter, and on this rock I will build My church, and the gates of Hades shall not prevail against it (Matt 16:18, NKJV).

Jesus declares that the gates of Hades will never overcome His Church. The Church of God is a mighty institution on the earth—vigorous, strong, firm and unyielding.

However, for many, the local church is a place of strife, narrow-mindedness and impoverished thinking. They see neither revival nor growth. Pastor and priest alike have formed their churches according to their own ideas and ambitions or the doctrines and expectations of their denominations. Churches vary in form, but they are commonly characterized by lack, defeat and worldly attitudes. This is not how God sees the Church.

> Simon Peter answered and said, "You are the Christ, the Son of the living God." Jesus answered and said to him, "Blessed are you, Simon Bar-Jonah, for flesh and blood has not revealed this to you, but My Father who is in heaven." And I also say to you that you are Peter, and on this rock I will build my church, and the gates of Hades shall not prevail against it. "And I will give you the keys of the kingdom of heaven, and whatever you bind on earth will be bound in heaven, and whatever you loose on earth will be loosed in heaven" (Matt 16:16-19, NKJV).

God views His Church entirely differently from the way we do. If we will receive His thoughts as revelation to our hearts, our churches will change, grow stronger and be far more effective. They will keep unity and harmony within and withstand the pressure and attacks of the devil without. Even in the most adverse circumstances, they will constantly increase. These will be militant churches, which determine and dominate the spiritual climate and stand uncompromisingly for the truth. They will involve all their members as workers, not spectators, and send missionaries to the ends of the earth. Such churches will be filled with a pure, holy and loving atmosphere where all who love Jesus and have bowed their hearts to Him and His conditions, not their own, will feel at home.

The Holy Spirit wants to show all believers today the potential and power of the local church. He wants to imprint the picture deep in your heart, so that you can see what the local church is, and what it can accomplish. When you see it, much will fall into place. You will find your place, your purpose in life, and your security and satisfaction there. Then, the gifts you have received from Him will reach their potential.

The Powerful Church

Romans 1:17 says, *The just shall live by faith.* Your personal life should be a life of faith. You must learn to walk by faith, live by faith, stand firm in the faith, overcome by faith and cast mountainous barriers into the sea by faith. God wants to teach you to put trust and confidence in Him so that your faith can be released to receive miracles in your life. Moreover, every believer must live his life somewhere and God has decided that place is in and through the local church.

You must, of course, spend time with God personally and take care that your inner life grows ever stronger with Him. However, "no man is an island" or lives a solitary life here on earth. You are set in a body of people, the Church. When true believers gather as a local church, things can happen which could never happen in or through *individual* believers *alone*.

In the past, mistaken teaching about the Church has immobilized its members and quenched many original initiatives. They have been checked, supervised, smothered, silenced and subdued. God does not want this.

When believers have the revelation of faith in their hearts, boundless initiative is released, enabling them to do the same things Jesus did (John 14:12). However, God does not want a lot of individualists following their own plans, independent of everyone else. We are all members of the same body (1 Cor 12:12,13). The place for unity, order and personal enterprise, freedom and uniqueness is *within* the local church. There, the individual and the communal combine to unleash mighty power from God.

The Boundless Church

In 1980 I was in Tulsa, Oklahoma, USA. When visiting Oral Roberts' University, the Lord said to me, "Look north, south, east and west." I did so and saw the stately buildings rising all around the Christian university campus. The Lord then said to me, "This is what I can do through *one* person who believes in me." Faith immediately flooded into me and filled my inner man. The realization exploded within me that "there really are no bounds" because, *all things are possible to him who believes* (Mark 9:23, NKJV).

Everything we have witnessed in Uppsala since then, can be traced back to what the Lord said to me in those few minutes.

I returned to Tulsa in the autumn of 1991. Before we left the city, I went to walk and pray on the university campus. There again, I sensed the presence of the Lord, but it was not until the flight home to Sweden that He spoke to me. His words were, "Just over 10 years ago I spoke to you about what one man can do who believes in me. Now I am talking to you again! There are no limits to what a church can do which is wholeheartedly devoted to me." His words sunk deeply into me. Individual men and women of God are wonderful and so are their achievements for Him. But in the End-times, they will be outshone by what God is doing through ordinary, but supernaturally equipped believers who have found their places in strong, growing, local churches.

We are entering the Last Days. They will be days of glory, confrontation and evangelism in the power of the Holy Spirit. But above all, they will be days when God restores His Church so it becomes what He planned, and fulfils His purpose. Today, the Church stands at the threshold of its height and glory.

Jesus, Lord of the Church

When Jesus speaks of His Church to Peter, He says, *Flesh and blood has not revealed this to you, but My Father who is in heaven* (Matt 16:17, NKJV). Peter realized that:

a) Jesus was the Messiah, the Anointed King, and as such must undoubtedly be the Son of God.

b) This revelation was the bedrock foundation of the Church.

c) The Church belongs to Jesus, and no one else.

d) The devil can never stop the Church if Jesus is allowed to decide how it is built.

All this came as revelation to Peter, and it is on this rock, this revelation, that Jesus will build His Church today. When we have the revelation that Jesus is the Messiah, we acknowledge Him as King, reigning in and through His Church. Therefore, every believer must bow in the obedience of faith to Him.

When a person is saved, he proclaims Jesus as his Lord (Rom 10:9). He *submits* his life to Jesus, and Jesus is the one who decides from then on. He is Master and Lord. I no longer decide—I follow Him.

At salvation, a person becomes a new creation in Christ Jesus (2 Cor 5:17). His sins are forgiven and his life is cleansed in Jesus' blood. He is included as a member in the body of Christ (1 Cor 12:13), the Church. The head of this body is Christ (Eph 1:22,23), and as head, Jesus makes the decisions.

When a believer joins a local church, he comes under the lordship of Jesus in that church. When I say, "Jesus is my Lord," I not only acknowledge Him as my personal Lord but as Lord in my church too. I submit to Him and His will and plans for that particular church. I align myself to what Jesus is doing in and through that church because He has placed me there. This does not create bondage. Instead, it results in great freedom.

Where Jesus is Lord, His Spirit is present, and where the Spirit is, there is liberty. Enterprise and initiative flow freely. Jesus is given true lordship and people are freed by their faithful obedience. Then, they can fulfill His plans for their lives.

No Place for Private Projects

The Church does not divest believers of their personal calling or God-given plans and enterprises. On the contrary, they come into them in earnest. There they are supported, developed and matured among the other members in the local church. The Church is no place for selfish ambitions or private empires.

There are always some people who leave the church complaining, "They wouldn't recognize me." Usually, it was simply the "ego" wanting recognition and support for its own ideas and projects. However, when their personal ambitions were not immediately received with welcoming arms, they turned around and left in a huff. Some people have even gone to the extent of spending years opposing, ridiculing, misrepresenting and slandering the situations they left in resentment and anger. How tragic! If such people are as anointed and spiritual as they claim, they should be able to take a challenge. Furthermore, they should not spend time defaming and opposing those they leave. Their behavior exposes the sin and ulterior motives behind their demands.

People will have to step over a higher threshold to join the churches of the future. At the same time, those who no longer want to comply with God's requirements and request to leave, will find it easy.

In churches like these, believers will discover that they have room to do all that the Lord has laid on their hearts.

The Vision—God's Directive to the Local Church

The foundation of any local church is *the vision* which Jesus has given it. This keeps it united and provides the motivating force for its members. Without vision or prophetic directive, *the people cast off restraint,* says Proverbs 29:18. Another translation puts it: *Where there is no vision the people perish* (KJV). Each vision is God's directive to a particular local church, defining its identity and work. It provides the blueprint for the special task God has given that church. His general will for all believers in every church can be read in the words of the Great Commission:

> Then Jesus came to them and said, "All authority in heaven and on earth has been given to me. Therefore go and make disciples of all nations, baptizing them in the name of the Father and of the Son and of the Holy Spirit, and teaching them to obey everything I have commanded you. And surely I will be with you always, to the very end of the age" (Matt 28:18-20).

Moreover, the Holy Spirit speaks to each church individually. In Habakkuk 2:1-3, the prophet says, *I will stand at my watch and station myself on the ramparts; I will look to see what he will say to me... Then the Lord replied: Write down the revelation and make it plain on tablets so that a herald may run with it. For the revelation awaits an appointed time; it speaks of the end and will not prove false. Though it linger, wait for it; it will certainly come and will not delay.*

Everything God does begins with a commission—a vision. Therefore, seek God until He answers. When He speaks, *write it down.* It should be easy to read and easy for everyone in the church to understand! Then they can hold on to that vision in their hearts and unity in the church will become a reality.

Unity does not simply mean that all are saved and have the Spirit of God. True unity is a working unity. Everyone is committed and moving forward in the same direction, working toward a common objective. This is more than just having my own needs met or my own ambitions fulfilled. This kind of unity is achieved when every church member has the one vision and task from the Holy Spirit in his heart. When that happens, frustration, confusion, obstinacy, fleshliness and worldliness leave. Everyone is agreed and committed to the word the Lord has given and wants nothing more than to see it fulfilled. God has promised that it will be fulfilled—but not tomorrow. It may take time but God promises, *"...wait for it; it will certainly come and will not delay."* When believers unite behind a distinct word from the Lord, they will have the joy of seeing His promises fulfilled before their eyes.

Heavenly Visions or Soulish Ambitions?

Nehemiah shows what is needed if the Lord is to give us a heavenly vision. There is a great difference between heavenly vision and soulish ambition. The entire book of Nehemiah reveals how God can use a believer with the right motives.

In the first chapter, Nehemiah weeps and prays because *the wall of Jerusalem is broken down, and its gates have been burned with fire* (Neh 1:3,4). His heart yearns for his people and longs for the restoration of his land. God sees it, and begins to use him.

Chapter two describes him alone, inspecting Jerusalem (vv 11-15). Having discovered its actual condition, he begins by addressing those *who did the work* (v 16). He says, *Come and let us build the wall of Jerusalem, that we may no longer be a reproach* (v 17). The leaders who were to cooperate with him replied, *"Let us rise up and build"* (v 18, NKJV).

This is how a pastor must always work. He cannot say, "I, me and mine," but, "We are going to build. Are you with us?" God deposits the vision in the heart of the shepherd, though never as his private property. The shepherd is simply the catalyst. He receives the vision from God, passes it on to the church and then leads the work. The vision belongs to the whole church. It is theirs, given them by God. As they all recognize the anointing on it and work to bring it to fulfilment, they will have immense satisfaction and joy. Then, the work of the Lord will be done and no one will be able to claim the glory for himself—God receives it all!

However, there are two pitfalls to avoid. One is the over-individualistic trap where everyone stares at the pastor and his vision. He may be powerful and anointed but he cannot possibly do everything himself, and he is certainly no Hollywood star around whom everything rotates. In such a church, built on personality instead of the word of the Lord, everything would stop as soon as the pastor was away. Such a church has no strength in itself. It is dependent on its "superstar" and is reminiscent of the world which lives through its film-stars, celebrities and heroes. They do all the work while we look on.

The other trap is to have a group which does not dare have a leader. All decide together and keep a check on each other. If one should accomplish more or receive more attention than another, envy arises. The book of Nehemiah shows how God puts a vision in the heart of one man. To achieve the vision, Nehemiah makes himself dependent on others and works together with them. But he does not abdicate from his position for fear of what people might think if he takes the lead and initiative. He works with others saying, "Come, let *us* build."

A Pattern for Every Church

The author of the book of Hebrews describes Moses' ministry and the heavenly tabernacle which was to be copied on earth. *Moses was **divinely instructed** when* *he was about to make the tabernacle. For He said, "See that you make all things according to the pattern shown you on the mountain"* (Heb 8:5, NKJV). God has a place *on the mountain* for all who seek Him. There, He will reveal the relevant pattern for each local church.

God shows His people *what* to do, *how* and *when* to do it and through *whom* it should be done! He then watches closely to see that His instructions are followed and that we do not invent our own or begin following anybody else's!

Vision is divine instruction received by revelation. Revelation is anointed by the Holy Spirit so, when we keep to the instructions the Lord has given by revelation, all will go well. The anointing and blessing are there, and where there is blessing and anointing the people will come! Of course, the devil hates any kind of revelation, not least vision in a local church. If it is working, he cannot split, secularize or stop it. So he will try to vex, bewilder, or distort God's plan and make a poor, weak copy by adding or subtracting from the original. But we have no authority to do this. Our job is to receive what the Lord has said, keep it and follow it exactly so that we "make all things according to the pattern shown ...on the mountain."

The Vision—a Heavenly Blueprint

Vision is not the same as passion. Passion is a heart on fire for something, for example, a land or a people. A vision is a clear and concise blueprint from heaven. This kind of description not only outlines what is to be built but also when, how and with whom. The vision itself may be very simple, consisting of only a few words, but through them the Lord clarifies how and when the vision should be carried out. Without this, there is no vision, only a notion.

When the Lord spoke to our church He gave us this vision: "Equip My people with My Word of faith, show them their spiritual weapons, train them how to use them and send them out in victorious battle for Me." This was God's directive and the foundation for all that we are doing today.

A great part of the vision concerns equipping and training people, so the whole church is affected. We have a Bible school, a prayer school, a music school, a missionary training school, Christian primary and high schools, and we are in the process of founding a Christian university. All this has come through the vision. This is also why we spread books, tapes and videos. Why? Because the Lord said so!

We must follow Paul who said, *Therefore, King Agrippa, I was not disobedient to the heavenly vision* (Acts 26:19, NKJV). When God speaks, you have to obey! If others dislike your obedience or the way in which you obey you must still obey! You will have to explain the vision and its content as best you can, and whether others obey or not, you have to set out regardless! In heaven, God will not ask, "What did everyone think of what I asked you to do?" but, "Did you do what I asked you?"

A directive from heaven transforms and fills the one who receives it. A church which receives a directive from God will be filled with an atmosphere of faith as the anointing on the calling comes over every member. However, this does not mean that everyone will be cast in the same mould. Different gifts and personalities will emerge in all their originality. But they will have the same spirit and thinking and the same objective behind them (Phil 1:27), creating prodigious strength and stability and releasing great energy.

This was what the Early Church was like. Every member had the same Lord, the same spirit, the same mind and the same goal. Acts 4:32 says, *All the believers were **one in heart and mind***. Great strength lies in such unity.

The Vision Attacked on All Sides

As God deposits a directive in the heart of a pastor and he shares it with his congregation, the whole church unites behind it. The vision has been imparted and brought to birth, but it has not yet reached full maturity. The devil hates this and he will immediately try to kill it. He attempts to destroy the vision through fear, division, envy, threat, slander and harassment. The stronger the word of the Lord, the hotter the opposition.

This was Nehemiah's experience. He suffered persistent persecution, threats, slander and blackmail attempts from Sanballat, Tobiah and Geshem (Neh 2:10, 2:19, 4:1-3, 4:7,8, 6:2-14).

Many others who have received words from the Lord have succumbed to such pressure, but not Nehemiah! He continued to build in spite of Sanballat's jeers, threats and animosity. Don't be distracted by the attacks of the enemy! Never fill your thoughts with what he is doing. What gets your attention gets you! Concentrate on the vision God has given you instead. Opposition will come but it cannot stop what God has promised. Never be afraid of persecution, gossip, or downright lies. Never be disappointed with other Christians who do not understand the vision or who openly fight it.

Before we began our work the Lord spoke to me through a prophet. He told me, "Some of those who are close to you now will openly oppose you later. Others who are afar off now will unite with you, and the work will be accomplished." This prophecy came first in 1982 and has been repeated since.

Revival history has always been the same. Some seem to be with you but their hearts are not. Others may at first oppose you but the Lord will touch their spiritual eyes so they begin to see. Therefore, never manipulate people. Do not bind them to you or coerce them to stay. Jesus never did. Never fear what might happen if all do not remain with you. God has called you. He will protect you and bring His work to completion.

The Vision Fulfilled

A divine vision can be fulfilled when it has:
  a) The right coworkers.
  b) The right motive.
  c) The right method.

d) The right resources.

All these areas will be challenged by the devil and you will have to live in faith for each of them. Do not "buy" coworkers.

The Bible says, *Like an archer who wounds at random is he who hires a fool or any passer-by* (Prov 26:10). You must trust God for the right assistants. Do not indiscriminately put anyone to the task just because of a need. Wait until the right person comes before initiating a new line of activity. When the right person comes, he will have the right motive and anointing for increase and victory. Such a person is like gold and will advance in the faith. The book of Proverbs says, *Do you see a man who excels in his work? He will stand before kings; He will not stand before unknown men* (Prov 22:29, NKJV).

Use spiritual methods that are filled with faith, not taken from this world and full of unbelief or manipulation. A right vision demands the right method or it will be impeded. Methods are not holy, so never idolize or worship them. They can be changed. But truths and principles from the Word of God are holy and never change. When movements stiffen and die, their followers commonly cling to outdated methods and refuse to change. Don't do that. Cling to the Word instead!

Your vision will cost money. Teach your congregation to believe God for both their own needs and the finances of their church. If God has said something, He will do it. However, it will always look impossible to the human eye and mind. God wants us to walk by faith for the projects He has given us. We were once wondering how we should meet the bill for something we wanted, when the Lord said, "What I order, I will pay for. What you order you can pay for." So make sure that what you are doing is ordered by heaven, not by your flesh! If it is from God, He will take care of it. Do not be depressed and worried or get ulcers over the church's finances. Just follow God's timetable for everything. Do not overdo things. Keep close to God and the finances will keep pace with you. Then your church will feel secure and witness many miracles.

2

Origins of the Church

And God placed all things under his feet and appointed him to be head over everything for the church, which is his body, the fullness of him who fills everything in every way (Eph 1:22,23).

When he referred to the Church, Paul was speaking of a mystery which had been revealed in the Last Days (Eph 1:9,10,22,23). During the Old Testament period, revelation on the Church was shrouded in mystery, for the time had not yet come for its appearance.

God chose to operate through His own peculiar people, Israel. Therefore, Gentiles had to go to Israel to partake of God's blessings. Mankind was then divided in two: Jews were in God's covenant, and Gentiles were outside God's covenant. However, in the fullness of time, God would extend His life, power and blessings to all mankind. Then, He would draw people from every tribe and nation into His Church.

The word "church" is *ekklesia* in Greek, meaning "called-out." In Greece, it also denoted the free citizens who were called out from the people to control the people. Now, through the Church, God calls men and women from every culture to fellowship with Him, work with Him, serve Him and lead together with Him.

The New Covenant—The Church Age

The price for all of mankind's sins was paid, through the death and resurrection of Jesus Christ. His blood provided a complete sacrifice for sins, and established the foundation for a new covenant. Jesus said, *This cup is the new covenant in my blood, which is poured out for you* (Luke 22:20).

The New Covenant did not erase the old covenant which God had made with His people, Israel. But now God includes people from all nations in the New Covenant. He is Lord of the whole earth, and the Gentiles should also praise His name! Now, the mystery would be revealed: *This mystery is that through the gospel the Gentiles are heirs together with Israel, members together of one body, and sharers together in the promise in Christ Jesus* (Eph 3:6).

When the Holy Spirit fell upon the disciples at Pentecost, Peter stood up and preached from Joel's prophecy concerning the phenomena of the Last Days. He described how the Spirit of God would be poured out on all people (Acts 2:17; Joel 2:28). There were two main implications. First, God's Spirit would no longer be over kings, priests and prophets exclusively, but over all believers. Second, God's Spirit would come over, not just the Jew, but the Greek (or the Gentile) as well.

The Church was born at Pentecost. A new people was created, consisting of individuals from every race, and the sign of this phenomenon was speaking in tongues. The disciples could now be heard speaking in tongues in many different languages, proclaiming the mighty deeds of God (Acts 2:11).

Thus, the Church Age began and the mystery was revealed. Through God's grace, the gospel of salvation would go throughout the world. All people, no matter what their position or background, could find salvation by calling on the name of Jesus, the Messiah. Simply by accepting the power and effect of Jesus' sacrificial death on the cross, and claiming His blood, they could receive total salvation. The Age of Grace, the Age of the New Covenant, had come!

The ancient Israelites in Egypt had access to salvation by streaking their doorposts with the blood of a lamb. This saved them from the Angel of Death. Later in the desert, they were bitten by snakes because of their sins. Then they looked up at the copper snake in faith, to heal them. Likewise, the Gentile can look in faith at Jesus on the cross, who became sin on his behalf, and he can receive salvation (2 Cor 5:21).

The Church—God's Channel of Blessing to All Mankind

Through the New Covenant, God came close to those who had once been far away (Eph 2:11-13). Those who had earlier been excluded, were now included. Those who were not previously a people, now became a people—the Church. This was not a new Israel, nor a people who substitute Israel, nor a covenant which replaces another, but something entirely new.

This is the Church, God's channel of blessing to all mankind during the Age of Grace. This age began on the Day of Pentecost with the outpouring of the Holy Spirit. It came through Jesus' reconciliatory death and resurrection, His victory over the devil, His ascension into heaven and return to the right side of the Father. His atoning death established the foundation for God's further dealings with man. Now, heaven is open for all the nations, allowing the blessings of Abraham to embrace all mankind. Anyone who believes, no matter what his origin, can partake of God's Spirit (Gal 3:13,14).

This was the revelation Peter received in Joppa. He was in Simon the tanner's house when he had the vision. Heaven opened, and a sheet bearing all kinds of animals was lowered. He heard a voice say, *"Get up, Peter. Kill and eat."* (Acts 10:9-13).

Afterwards, Peter went to Caesarea, to the home of a centurion, Cornelius, who had received an angelic vision. When Peter preached to these Gentiles, the Holy Spirit came over them and they began speaking in tongues (Acts 10:44-46). Then Peter said, *"I now realise how true it is that God does not show favoritism but accepts men from every nation who fear him and do what is right,"* and that, *"everyone who believes in him receives forgiveness of sins through his name"* (Acts 10:34,35,43).

This revelation of the sheet bearing the clean and unclean animals, and Cornelius' subsequent conversion, opened the door to the Gentile nations. For them, the way to God was through faith in Jesus, not through the law and circumcision. This was what Paul contested for all his life. He did not strive to abolish the law, but maintained that it was unnecessary for Gentiles to first undergo circumcision in order to come to God.

Now, through Jesus' sacrificial death, the Gentile races could come direct to God apart from the law, circumcision and temple service. Circumcision was a sign of the Abrahamic Covenant for the Jewish people. Paul never said that the Jews should abolish circumcision. According to Scripture, it was an everlasting sign of the covenant between them and God (Gen 17:13). Paul meant that the Gentiles need not circumcise themselves to be accepted by God. However, both the circumcised Jew and the uncircumcised Gentile must believe in God for their justification:

> For we maintain that a man is justified by faith apart from observing the law. Is God the God of Jews only? Is he not the God of the Gentiles too? Yes, of Gentiles too, since there is only one God, who will justify the circumcised by faith and the uncircumcised through that same faith (Rom 3:28-30).

Jews comprised the original membership of the Early Church. They were all Messianic Jews, those Jews who believed that Jesus, *Yeshua,* was the Messiah, *ha Mashiah.* They were all pierced to the heart and turned away from their sins (Acts 2:37,38). All received the Holy Spirit and were born again, and became new creations as God's Spirit created in them a new person.

For these Jews, salvation did not imply conversion to a new religion. They received the prophetic promises concerning the Messiah and His deeds, and the outpouring of the Holy Spirit. They knew God's Spirit would be put in them and they would all know the Lord (Ezek 36:27; Jer 31:33,34). Yet they still had to study the law, keep the Sabbath, go to the temple, observe prayer times, hold the various celebrations and circumcise their male infants. Nowhere was it written that they should stop doing this.

Still, in all these observances there were two things they should also do: a) accept Jesus, the Messiah whom God had sent, and b) spread the good news about Him to all people. Jesus had commanded His disciples to go out into all the world. This was remarkable for a Jew who did not want to make himself unclean by associating with heathens. But now the Age of Grace had come and God was seeking the Gentiles. He would establish this through the Church, which now comprised both Jew and Gentile who confessed Jesus as the Messiah, Savior. Eventually, as the gospel went out, Gentile converts far outnumbered their Jewish counterparts. But the Scriptures emphasize that the gospel *is the power of God to salvation for everyone who believes, for the Jew first and also for the Greek* (Rom 1:16, NKJV).

The Church—Born and Growing in the Supernatural

When the apostles began to preach the gospel, God confirmed it with signs and wonders. The Church was birthed in the supernatural and grew in the supernatural. Throughout the Roman Empire, people could hear the gospel and see God performing miracles to confirm it.

This was exactly what Jesus had promised His disciples: *But you will receive power when the Holy Spirit comes on you; and you will be my witnesses in Jerusalem, and in all Judea and Samaria, and to the ends of the earth* (Acts 1:8). That power was confirmed by the gospel.

Paul also testifies of this: *I will not venture to speak of anything except what Christ has accomplished through me in leading the Gentiles to obey God by what I have said and done—by the power of signs and miracles, through the power of the Spirit. So from Jerusalem all the way round to Illyricum, I have proclaimed the gospel of Christ* (Rom 15:18,19).

When the Spirit came on the Day of Pentecost, God sanctioned this new age with a tremendous explosion of power. The disciples were filled with boldness. They used the sword of the gospel to cut through all prejudice and limitations, all opposition and hate, and loudly proclaimed freedom for captives throughout the Roman Empire. The time of bondage was over. The debt was paid and sin was atoned for. The power of death was broken and Satan was defeated! Forgiveness, peace, righteousness, healing and deliverance were now available to all mankind, through faith in Jesus. Wherever the disciples preached and proclaimed this, God confirmed it with signs and wonders. Crowds of people were saved, healed of diseases and delivered from evil spirits.

The same deeds which Jesus performed when He *went around doing good and healing all who were under the power of the devil, because God was with him* (Acts 10:38), were done by His disciples everywhere: *Then the disciples went out and preached everywhere, and the Lord worked with them and confirmed his word by the signs that accompanied it* (Mark 16:20). Everywhere the disciples went, people were healed and delivered, breaking loose from Satan's chains and fetters. New churches were established and strengthened by the teaching. Consequently, new believers started to go out and proclaim Jesus as Lord, declaring that, the gospel *is the power of God to salvation for everyone who believes* (Rom 1:16, NKJV).

The Church—A Willing Instrument for the Holy Spirit

The Early Church was characterized by many different qualities:

1. *Obedience.* Jesus was accepted as Messiah and Lord.

2. *Glory.* God's Spirit was working within and through the Church. The Church was filled with God's presence and became His dwelling-place in the Spirit (Eph 2:21,22).

3. *Signs and Wonders*. Supernatural manifestations were common. There were miracles, healings and deliverances. Believers received revelations, visions, angelic visitations, prophecies, and words of knowledge and wisdom. The supernatural was the norm, and not considered as something odd. The gifts of the Spirit were evident and God continually performed miracles.

4. *Faith*. God was always expected to intervene and do the impossible, and so He did. He delivered Peter, halted opposition, brought Tabitha back to life, and shook the jail in Philippi to set Paul free.

5. *Teaching*. The apostles taught the believers daily, so that they became strong in the Word, followed sound doctrine, and grew in understanding and wisdom.

6. *God's Ordinances*. The believers knew their place and flowed with one another in the ministry gifts, with elders and deacons. The ministry gifts were free to fulfill their purpose—to build up the body of Christ. They could minister to the believers, under the power and anointing of the Holy Spirit (Eph 4:11-13).

In other words, Jesus was Lord of His Church, and the gates of hell could not overpower it. The Holy Spirit, whose dwelling-place in the present age is the Church, could take control and flow freely within her. Therefore, she became a ready instrument in His hands. Through the Church, the gospel could reach out in power and touch nation after nation. This was her ultimate purpose—to preach the gospel to all mankind.

Success always accompanies the Word! This is not historic or strange, but normal, biblical Christianity, and God's pattern for every congregation. When He was on earth, Jesus preached and taught with signs and miracles. He still wants to do this through His Church which is His body on earth today. Jesus has not changed. The gospel has not changed. The Church has not changed.

The Growing Church Meets Opposition

The Church's explosive beginning triggered shock waves in the spirit world. The devil and his troops were forced to retreat, but it did not take long before they retaliated. Their first counterattack was to incite persecution *because of the word* (Mark 4:17). Consequently, the disciples' work was opposed, and they were despised, persecuted, thrown into prison and executed. But the more the Church was persecuted, the more power it received. Persecution was closely followed by greater wisdom, signs and wonders. The Church grew as increasing numbers of bold believers joined the faith.

Some believers have thought that the gospel can spread without persecution—but that is unbiblical. They gladly welcome the signs and wonders described in Acts, but leave out the opposition and persecution which are also part of the picture. You cannot have one without the other. Nonetheless, Paul encourages us in Romans 8:37: *In all these things we are more than conquerors through him who loved us.*

There is victory over opposition and persecution. In the midst of it all, there is protection and a way out. However, it is completely unbiblical to assume that the world will favor the gospel and raise no objections. Jesus was clear when He said, *"In this world you will have trouble. But take heart! I have overcome the world"* (John 16:33). Jesus prayed for His disciples to His Father, saying, *I have given them your word and the world has hated them, for they are not of the world any more than I am of the world* (John 17:14).

We should pray for opportunities and favor with people, and walk in love toward all people. Then many will see Jesus in us, like what they see, and be saved. But meanwhile, do not forget that the spirit of this world is the spirit of Antichrist and it does not love us. Satan, the god of this age, hates us and our work. We will not find favor with him, unless we are acting in error and compromising with the world.

Satan Attacks the Church
through Worldliness and Religiosity

When Satan's head-on attacks fail, he uses another tactic, and tries to penetrate the Church from within. These subtle attacks come mainly from two directions:

a) The world and worldliness.

b) Religion and religiosity.

Both strategies have a common goal—to strip the Church of her power and initiative.

The Church was born in the supernatural and functions in the supernatural. Furthermore, she has been equipped with spiritual weapons: *For the weapons of our warfare are not carnal but mighty in God for pulling down strongholds* (2 Cor 10:4, NKJV). Her strength lies in the Spirit, not the flesh. When a church functions and flows in the Spirit, God's power and presence are there. But when a church reacts out of the flesh, it sinks to the same level as the world, and loses its ability to penetrate and influence.

A believer can be born again and possess God's Spirit yet continue to live through his soul and his flesh. This is also true of a church. True strength is found neither in the body nor in the soul, but in the Spirit. Soulish strength, emotions, reason and will-power are not enough. Physical strength alone will not suffice.

If a believer does not draw from life in the Spirit, and strength from the Spirit's wisdom, he will never live in victory, function in the supernatural and experience breakthrough and success. This also applies to the local church. Therefore, the enemy has tried to seduce her with worldliness, so that she is ultimately stripped of her power.

Worldliness saps the Church of her strength, but so too, does religion. The great persecutions against Christianity persisted up to the beginning of the fourth century, when attitudes toward the Church changed drastically. The State authorities, led by the new Emperor, Constantine, realized that it was impossible to obliterate Christianity, as the former Roman Emperors had aimed. Instead, they did a complete turn. First, Christianity was tolerated, then it became an imposed State religion. The Christian faith was now a prerequisite for recruitment to an official post. People were attracted to the Church— but not for the right reasons. It was not conviction of sin or longing for salvation that drew them to the Church, but the desire to be "in." It became expedient to be a Christian! Before long, this maneuver took effect and both the Church and the gospel became altered and distorted.

As a result of these attacks, the Church became something totally different to what is described in the New Testament. Spiritual authority was replaced by political and religious power. Spiritual and ministerial gifts were replaced by the sacraments and the offices of Church politics. In place of the supernatural came superstition and human ideas about peace. Instead of power in the gospel came human traditions which were handed down from generation to generation. Instead of life, came death. The Church became shrouded in a thousand years of darkness, which Luther later described as the "Babylonian captivity of the Church."

3

A Bird's-eye View
of Church History

"But you will receive power when the Holy Spirit comes on you; and you will be my witnesses in Jerusalem, and in all Judea and Samaria, and to the ends of the earth" (Acts 1:8).

We cannot comprehend the Lord's plans with the Church today without first understanding its history. Since her birth nearly 2,000 years ago, the Church has grown and spread the gospel throughout the world.

Even first generation Christians succeeded in taking the gospel to all the known world.

All over the world this gospel is producing fruit and growing, just as it has been doing among you since the day you heard it and understood God's grace in all its truth (Col 1:5,6).

The gospel was proclaimed in every social group and class, reaching even "Caesar's household" (Phil 4:22).

Christianity Becomes a State Religion

As long as persecution persisted, the Church remained united and focused on the essentials. Believers had no choice but to depend upon God for everything, and a high cost followed a commitment to Jesus. Their sacrifices, however, were so pleasing to God that He sent the fire of the Holy Spirit over His people. The Church was alive in the supernatural and experienced continuous growth.

Roman resistance eventually weakened, and the whole situation changed with Emperor Constantine. In AD 313, he introduced an edict of tolerance whereby Christianity was officially accepted as a valid religion among others. Christians were granted retribution for their losses, and even confiscated property and possessions were returned to them. All this seemed wonderful—the era of persecution and martyrdom had finally ended. But now the trend took a different turn.

Christianity was not only recognized, but became the official religion. Only professing Christians could attend public meetings and hold a government office. Christianity was the key to finding a respectable position in society and was even compulsory for citizenship and for conducting business. Prestige and power now became part of the picture.

Church leaders, who already had considerable status, gained greater prominence as they assumed roles as Church barons, negotiating with State officials.

But as difficulties arose in determining where the borders between Church and State should be drawn, greed and selfish ambition motivated the inevitable power struggles. Thus, political influence and power accompanied spiritual leadership, and spiritual weapons became carnal. A strong, centralized system of control took over and the Church gradually changed.

Acceptance by the State had led to corruption by the State. New Testament Christianity, with its intrinsic teaching, power and order, began to alter and deteriorate. In its place, there emerged a bureaucratic religious machine operating in coalition with the State. Of course, the Bible was quoted and Jesus was confessed as the Church's Lord, but beneath lay a powerful blend of religiosity and worldliness.

Man is Incurably Religious

Man is a religious being. He is created to have communion with God and to live spiritually in harmony with Him. Then God fulfills his needs, and both God and man live and work together. In this way, man's life is filled with God's life and glory. When man's relationship with his Creator is right, his spirit is alive, and he honors and glorifies God, who is central.

All this was man's privilege before the Fall, but through the Fall everything changed. Man became a sinner and lost the glory of God (Rom 3:23). God's response to this was the gospel. God's solution was to send His Son, Jesus, as a sacrifice of reconciliation for the sins of mankind. Man, through faith, accepts God's gift and his relationship with God is restored. God's solution is free, a gift of grace. Man simply needs to receive it by faith.

Religiosity is totally different. It is man's own efforts to create a platform from which he believes he can have a relationship with God. It does not come through revelation from God, but through man's own experience, reasoning, will and traditions.

Many believers may be surprised to see that fleshliness and worldliness can don religious clothing, but is this really so strange? Man is incurably religious, even when his spirit has not been awakened by God's Spirit. An unrepentant individual, who has not seen his miserable condition as a sinner, nor received grace as an undeserved gift, can certainly be religious.

Religion Leads to Sin and Rebellion

Every person who does not have peace with God has a troubled conscience, so he seeks to relieve it or to bargain with it. Adam covered his nakedness with fig leaves after losing God's glory (Gen 3:7). This is precisely what religion is: man's own meager attempts through religious deeds, ideas and traditions to hide his nakedness before God. Instead, he should acknowledge his own inability to save himself and surrender himself to God's mercy.

This basic condition has given rise to every form of religion, witchcraft and occultism in the world. Deep inside, man has longed for God since he lost his relationship with Him. He searches everywhere and is never fulfilled. Since the inner, spirit man is dead he seeks with his soul and body. He strives through his desires, emotions and reason in vain, for the soul produces neither spiritual life nor peace. This can only come from God through the new birth (John 3:3-5).

Man's striving for God is an inherent part of his carnal nature, so problems will naturally arise as he seeks peace without humbling himself. But God gives peace in His way and on His conditions, not man's.

A person may want salvation and righteousness, but if he is not prepared to humble himself and receive it in God's way, he lives in sin and rebellion. He lives with his own self-righteousness and "salvation"—but this can never be accepted or blessed by God. Jesus said:

> "'These people honor me with their lips, but their hearts are far from me. They worship me in vain; their teachings are but rules taught by men.' You have let go of the commands of God and are holding on to the traditions of men." And he said to them: "You have a fine way of setting aside the commands of God in order to observe your own traditions!" (Mark 7:6-9).

Paul spoke about the consequences of such behavior: *having a form of godliness but denying its power"* (2 Tim 3:5). This is the veneer of manmade religion which, although laced with prayers and scriptures, comes from an unrepentant heart. The person who has such a hypocritical relationship with God, refuses to relinquish what he has, and justifies his own righteousness. In his heart there is no sincere doing away with sin and rebellion, or obedience through repentance and faith.

If this continues, he opens himself to the influence of religious demons who entice him toward witchcraft and occultism. This is simply the endeavor to find supernatural power, knowledge and prestige for oneself, rather than walking in God's ways. Consequently, such people come under the influence of evil spirits. They may even get some of their powers, but in fact they are driven and manipulated by these spirits.

The Bible warns us against getting involved in any form of witchcraft or occultism (Lev 19:26, 20:6; Deut 18:9-12). Paul states in 1 Cor 10:20:

No, but the sacrifices of pagans are offered to demons, not to God, and I do not want you to be participants with demons.

There are elements of witchcraft and occultism in all forms of religion. Man's efforts, traditions, and religious ideas fail to gain access to God. Therefore he is compelled, through sin and religious pride, to crack the barriers to the supernatural through the occult. There he hopes to find the fulfilment he seeks, along with spiritual experiences, religious prestige and power. The gospel alone is the *power of God* to salvation, and it stands in direct opposition to man's religion.

The Religious World Opposes Revival

In all revivals the greatest opposition to God's work does not come from the secular world, but from the religious world. When God's light, revelation and power come, even religion is unmasked. Unlike the world, religion claims to be associated with spiritual affairs. Religiosity wants to monopolize the things of God, and so its exposure is far more drastic.

Revival must strip religion. This is not intentionally directed at individuals, but toward the ideas and systems. There are sincere people who seek and long for God, but they are suffocating in religious rules and regulations. God wants to release such people, and destroy the structure which hinders them from experiencing the freedom and power of the gospel.

After Christianity was accepted by the State, it became distorted. Doctrines on grace, faith, repentance and salvation were perverted. Repentance from the heart and the new birth were no longer emphasized. People believed that God's grace was obtained through the sacraments— infant baptism, communion, confirmation, confession, marriage, priesthood, ordination and finally, extreme unction. These external ceremonies were supposed to be channels for God's grace.

One could only become a Christian by doing all these things! The most important of these sacraments was infant baptism. It was taught that an infant was born again through water baptism, as God's Spirit was imparted through the water. If the child continued to live according to the Church system, and participated in the various sacraments, then the child was a Christian. But the Word, preaching and repentance were not given priority.

Ordinary "lay men" had no access to the Scriptures. This was reserved for priests who also had the exclusive rights to their interpretation. Assurance of salvation was never mentioned, probably because the priests, who were usually unsaved men, lacked that assurance themselves. How then, could a person be sure of going to heaven? He couldn't, of course, but he could hope for God's acceptance if he were faithful enough in carrying out and receiving the various sacraments. This resulted in an enormous doctrine of works which combined various occult elements.

As man strove for holiness, peace and God's acceptance, he formed "holy orders" and "holy places," with "holy objects," "saints" and so on. All these were nothing more than man's contrived attempts to reach God and obtain His approval. He did not realize that these means undermined God's work through Christ on the cross, who once and for all reconciled mankind to Himself.

Official Christianity developed in a disgusting way. Many superstitions began to flourish together with the worship of saints, fetishes, fables, myths and unbiblical traditions. As the outer power of the Church and its grandeur increased, its inner power diminished. Biblical revelation was withheld from the people, who were lost in a maze of condemnatory fabrications and superstitious beliefs. Reverence for God and a holy life-style were replaced by liturgy, pilgrimages, flagellation, monks and holy orders. Candles and crucifixes became holy objects. Icons became an occult medium through which, it was said, life and grace were imparted from heaven. As the papacy developed, so too did the worship of saints (ancestor worship), and Mariology. Latin became a holy language and the liturgy was read with Latin prayers, like occult incantation.

In the midst of this were people who genuinely loved and longed for God, but they were often persecuted, despised and rejected, if not tortured and burned at the stake. The religion which had developed was, at its best, a parody of New Testament Christianity, and at its worst, a demonic imitation devised to extinguish the power and life from the Church of the living God. Spiritual darkness now engulfed the so-called Christian world.

Two groups of people were particularly targeted for the wrath of this harlot church: Christians who spoke for revival, and the Jews.

True to a harlot's nature, the backslidden State Church was quick to embrace anti-Semitism. This same venomous hatred, which has always sought to destroy God's people, the Jews, and rob them of His promises, now began working through the State Church. Even today, vehement anti-Semitic teaching and practice remains in so-called Christian associations. In these circles, there has always been a hatred for both the genuine Christian life in the living Church and for God's own people, the Jews.

The backslidden Church had stolen and imitated what God had given to both the Jewish people and the living Church. Moreover, she clothed herself with political power and amassed tremendous wealth through monopolization. Wherever she has been, she has sought to persecute and quench genuine spiritual life.

For almost one thousand years, the Church was enslaved, duped and buried in this spiritual darkness. The devil had succeeded in obscuring much of what belonged to true, godly living. Meanwhile, however, the Lord had preserved His *seven thousand men who had not bowed down to Baal* (1 Kings 19:18). Throughout Church history there have been oases of freedom, blessings and revival. However, the cost was high for those faithful people who honored God and refused to compromise with the degenerate Church.

The Reformation—The Church's Restoration

The start of the 16th Century brought a movement that would revolutionize the whole world and open the way to the restoration of the Church. The Reformation continues today and will not cease until full restoration is achieved, and God's Church becomes all that He has intended it to be.

The Reformation totally shattered the dominant Church and the Dark Ages it had shaped. It began with one man's experience with God—Martin Luther (1483-1546). We do not need much insight to see his shortcomings and to conclude that he did not have a complete revelation of God's will in certain areas. However, we need to understand the spiritual poverty of his time to appreciate Luther's great spiritual courage. He sparked the flame of the Reformation and fanned it into fire. At one stage, he stood alone against the whole world, and the repercussions were far-reaching. The Church's liberation from "Babylonian captivity" had begun.

Martin Luther

As a monk, Luther was deeply anchored in Catholicism with all its teachings on works, superstitions, human traditions and Church politics. In spite of this, there was one unanswered question which dogged Luther: "How does one have peace with God?" or "How does one find a God of mercy?"

For Luther and his contemporaries, God was perceived as wrathful and incalculable, an unapproachable judge whom one had to appease. Luther had a sensitive conscience—some say over-sensitive! He did everything he could to earn God's mercy but his life became even more miserable. As a monk, priest, and later Professor of Theology, he religiously fasted and prayed to Mary and the saints. He wore horsehair shirts, made regular confessions and pilgrimages, and bought indulgences, hoping to find peace with God. But it was futile!

His confessor, Staupitz, asked him why he could not be like all the others and just accept that he was a sinner. If he tried his best, God would probably receive him. Yet that was precisely what he could not accept. In his conscience he felt that God was against him. However much he tried, it just did not seem to be enough. Mere resignation promised no peace either. Whichever way he turned, there was no solution to this impossible dilemma. No priest could tell him that he already had forgiveness— he knew he had no peace with God.

During this period Luther visited Rome, Christianity's capital. He staunchly prayed, fasted and gave alms. He even walked on his knees praying on Sancta Scala. These were the holy stairs where, according to tradition, Jesus stood when he was sentenced to crucifixion by Pilate. Luther saw and touched the holy relics, and did everything in his power to please God through these sacred "touchings." Yet he remained empty inside. At the same time, he noticed the spiritual, moral and political decadence of Rome, and returned to Germany even more disheartened.

Soon, Luther became Professor of Theology at the new Wittenberg University where he lectured on Psalms, Romans and Galatians. One day, as he studied Romans 1:16,17, he experienced a profound revelation which came like a flash of lightning.

> I am not ashamed of the gospel, because it is the power of God for the salvation of everyone who believes: first for the Jew, then for the Gentile. For in the gospel a righteousness from God is revealed, a righteousness that is by faith from first to last, just as it is written: "The righteous will live by faith."

The veil over his understanding suddenly lifted. He realized that righteousness, peace, justification and mercy were *not* earned through *man's* efforts or religious deeds. They are imparted by God through Christ's sacrifice on the cross. Everything he has done *for us* on the cross, He works *in us* when we receive *by faith* His gift of salvation through Christ Jesus. *For we maintain that a man is justified by faith apart from observing the law* (Rom 3:28).

Luther had experienced forgiveness through grace, and the revelation that he could simply *receive* everything through Christ entirely changed his life. It not only changed his life, but also ignited a revolution which would eventually transform all Europe and spread throughout the world.

Luther gradually became aware that the whole religious system to which he belonged was obsolete. At first, he only intended to reform the Church on a few points. However, without realizing it, he had started to expose a gigantic religious system which not only held millions of people in bondage, but also blocked their way to salvation and life with God.

He began to realize that the Church had totally perverted the gospel. The gospel of grace had been replaced by legalistic works. Faith had been substituted by superstition and religious actions. The Bible had been replaced by human legends, traditions and the Canon Law. Instead of the outworkings of the Word and the Spirit through ministerial gifts, there were popes, cardinals and priests whose word took precedence over the Bible.

Selling indulgences was, above all, particularly loathsome to Luther. This was probably the most misguided path in the entire labyrinth of heresy. The Church taught that monks and priests could be paid to pray for the souls of the dead. This was supposed to release them from purgatory, the so-called state of suspension between heaven and hell. In this way, much money was extorted from the simple people. The Pope proclaimed a special indulgence called "Peter's penny" which was used to build St. Peter's in Rome. Through this indulgence, a deceased relative was supposedly saved from years of suffering in purgatory. This fabrication of heresy and greed exploited the people's spiritual ignorance. Furthermore, it aggravated the problem of sin in people's lives instead of helping them find relief through the power of the Word.

Luther protested by nailing 95 theses to the church door at Castle Church, Wittenberg, on 31 October 1517. Through this, he challenged the dogma of indulgence, and sought a discussion on this and other controversial matters. The Reformation was born! Within a few months, the fire of revolution broke out and spread throughout Europe. As events unfolded, Luther's arguments grew more radical: of course the Pope and his Church councils could err—the Bible alone was the final authority. A drastic development followed.

Luther was consequently excommunicated and outlawed. When the papal bull of excommunication arrived, Luther responded by burning it along with the whole Canon Law. The grip of Catholicism over Europe was now loosened, giving way to the rise and growth of Protestant churches everywhere.

The Reformation was a restoration of teaching rather than a revival, although thousands of people heard the truth and finally found peace with God. Luther, also translated the Bible from Latin to German, so the former language eventually became obsolete. Gutenberg's printing press worked at top speed as Bibles, tracts, complementary books, psalms and songs were widely distributed, providing the people with the gospel for the first time. Luther wrote psalms which were sung everywhere, and it is said these psalms did more to spread the gospel throughout Europe than the actual sermons he preached.

Luther summarized the main points of his doctrine thus:

1. Sola gracis—by grace alone. What God has done through Christ is sufficient.

2. Sola fide—by faith alone. Your duty is to believe, not to work for your salvation.

3. Sola scriptura—the Word alone. The highest and final authority in a Christian's life is the Bible, not the word of popes and bishops.

4. Sola Christo—through Christ alone. He is the Bible's heart and focus, and the center of all Christian life and

faith. He is the model and example for the church. He alone is enough.

The Reformation which Luther began split Europe. One religious skirmish after another broke out but no one could stop the Reformation. The movement was now too strong and widespread. Other leaders of the same spirit arose and carried the torch further—Calvin, Zwingli, Bucer and Knox. In the midst of medieval superstition, the authority of the Scriptures and the truth of justification were emblazoned like strong banners on a mountain top. No one could destroy this revelation—a restoration of teaching had begun.

John Wesley

A few hundred years later, the Lord used another man, John Wesley (1703-1791), to re-establish the concept of holy living. Wesley was an Englishman and an Anglican priest with a theological education. He had preached for several years and even worked as a missionary among North American Indians before experiencing his own salvation.

His salvation took place on 24 May 1738 (at the age of 35) while listening to a reading of Luther's preface to Romans. He described the moment thus: "About a quarter before nine, when he was describing the change which God works in the heart through faith in Christ, I felt my heart strangely warmed. I felt I did trust in Christ, Christ alone, for salvation; and an assurance was given me that He had taken away my sins, even mine, and saved me from the law of sin and death."

After the Reformation, Protestant Europe underwent industrialization. The Reformation had laid the foundation for its development, rejecting superstition and clearing the way for scientific progress.

Men now appealed to human conscience saying that the Bible should be read in the light of individual conscience. They also challenged each other to use their God-given sensibility to explore, investigate, develop and conserve the world God had given them. In Protestant Europe, a significant development took place socially, economically, and politically. The Bible, the Ten Commandments and the Christian faith became the foundation of society, affecting legislation and education.

However, the spiritual fire of the Reformation eventually died down to empty, pedantic debates on theological doctrines. "Faith" was so over-emphasized that it came to mean that it made no difference how one lived since one was saved by grace and not by works. At the same time, the intellectuals of that era entertained notions from various philosophers, including rationalism, deism and atheism. Both faith and doubt became intellectual. Rationalism, with its skeptical approach to anything which could not be grasped intellectually, began to apply its critique to certain aspects of biblical teaching.

While the Reformation confronted tradition, the revival of the 18th century confronted rationalism and worldliness. Wesley, who had been born again, saw the difference between heart-faith and mere intellectual confession. It was not sufficient to accept or tolerate biblical doctrine with the mind alone. A genuine, deep faith was needed which expressed itself through holy living.

This led to revelation on two important truths concerning the believer's life:

1. One must be born again (John 3:3-5).

2. As a true believer who has experienced the new birth, one must then live a consecrated, holy life.

The new birth and holiness were emphasized as never before. Established religion, which was permeated by "rational thinking" and worldliness, strongly resisted this revelation.

Wesley faced persecution for almost all his life. His followers, who were called Methodists after their spiritually disciplined lives, grew by the thousands. The Methodist Revival spread throughout Europe and North America and made an impact on society, especially in England, which was beset with social misery, chaos and poverty. Many believed that the French Revolution would spread to England, but this never occurred. France was the only Catholic country in Europe which had a strong revival (the Huguenot Revival). Yet it failed to overthrow Catholic domination, and reaped the terror of the Revolution. England, on the other hand, reaped a revival which swept through the land and reached thousands of impoverished coalminers, leaving marked improvements in social conditions.

Two things resulted from this revival:
a) Social awareness and compassion.
b) Evangelization and mission.

Revelation on salvation, holy living, helping the poor, and missions for winning the lost had far-reaching effects.

The established churches, Catholic as well as Protestant, had assumed that infant baptism automatically made Christians of people in a "Christian" country, unless they professed otherwise. Now the revelation had come that you had to be born again. You, as an individual, had to turn away from the sin in your life and repent. You had to receive Jesus in your heart, before God, and live in holy service for Him.

Revelation on godly living as opposed to teaching alone, was also firmly anchored in the Church as the restoration progressed.

The Pentecostal Revival

The third area of restoration we will examine is that of God's power. The Church in the book of Acts had sound biblical teaching and true revelation which gave people freedom and restoration. Christians lived holy, surrendered lives, but they had also been equipped from above with the Holy Spirit's power. When the Church later fell into false religiosity and worldliness, its power disappeared. God operates in the supernatural, through signs and wonders, but this can only come where faith and holiness are present. Not even Jesus, the only Son of God, could perform any powerful miracles in Nazareth apart from healing a few of the sick: *And he was amazed at their lack of faith* (Mark 6:6).

During the course of the Church's history, the perception of God had altered. From being a good, loving father, He was perceived as a wrathful, unpredictable judge. His willingness and ability to heal were underestimated. Instead of standing on His Word and receiving healing in faith, people turned instead to amulets, fetishes, holy places and occult rites. Biblical accounts of healing were thought to be irrelevant for the present dispensation. Worse still, rationalism declared them to be mere fables. Such an atmosphere was hardly inviting for the Holy Spirit to manifest His signs and wonders. But the Lord started to change that spiritual climate by restoring both doctrine and life-styles.

A new revival came at the beginning of the 20th century—the Pentecostal Revival. This marked the beginning of the re-establishment of God's power in the Church. This did not take place through a particular person who acted as the leader, but appeared and developed in several places and spread throughout the world. If there is a single person who stands in the center of this revival, He must be the third person in the Trinity, God the Holy Spirit.

This revival began when believers longed for more power in the supernatural, to experience the signs and wonders of which the Bible speaks. A Methodist, Charles Parnham, started a Bible school in Topeka, Kansas, USA, where believers devoted themselves to the study of the baptism of the Spirit. They saw the connection between the gift of tongues and the baptism of the Holy Spirit, realizing that tongues were an outer manifestation and sign of this. The Bible students began to seek this, and the first manifestation of the Spirit's baptism with tongues came on New Year's Day, 1901.

The new century began with a blessing. The Church was now empowered to go to the ends of the earth to reap the last harvest before the Lord returns.

From Topeka, the teaching and experience of the Spirit's baptism spread to Houston, Texas, where Parnham started a Bible school. One of the students who had to sit outside to listen because he was black—the South was still segregated then—took the teaching to Los Angeles. In 1906, the Azuza Street Revival broke out. Over the next three years, people gathered from all over the world to pray, seek God, be baptized in the Holy Spirit and pray in tongues. Many miracles took place, and believers carried this fire to different countries where the Pentecostal Revival rapidly spread.

As was the case with the Reformation and the Methodists, the Pentecostal Revival was persecuted and ridiculed. But no matter how the devil tried to obstruct God's power, he could not stop the powerful outpouring of God's Spirit which inaugurated the 20th century. Eventually, even that revival began to grow stale in some areas. However, the Spirit's work progressed through the Healing Revival, the Charismatic Revival, various prophetic movements, and the Faith Movement.

Believers began to understand and appreciate the Holy Spirit as never before. They began to understand the gifts of the Spirit with their various supernatural manifestations, and even anticipated signs and wonders. They prayed for the sick and cast out demons. They started to prophesy and receive supernatural insight. Supernatural power, supernatural wisdom and the supernatural presence of God were no longer considered strange. They recognized the believer's duties and inherent authority. All believers could speak in tongues. All—not just priests and theologians—could be led by God's Spirit and heal the sick and cast out evil spirits (Mark 16:17-20).

All believers have authority and dominion in Jesus' name. They can expect answers to prayer and miracles in His name. They can resist Satan and see him flee in Jesus' name. All these biblical truths were not operating in fullness at the beginning of the revival. However, they were gradually revealed during the 20th century, and they have, in part, been re-established in the Church. The main doctrines which characterized this revival were:

1. Jesus saves.
2. Jesus baptizes in the Holy Spirit.
3. Jesus heals and delivers.
4. Jesus' return is imminent.

A strong wave of mission coupled with great anticipation of signs and wonders emerged from this revival, which has progressed through various phases of revelation. This is the current spiritual climate in which the modern Church dwells.

The Greatest Revival in World History

Smith Wigglesworth was one of the spiritual pioneers in the early years of this century. Before he died, he received a prophetic message which revealed the progression of the Spirit's work. (At that time it looked as if it was about to ebb away.) A revival with powerful miracles and healings would come. And it did come after Wigglesworth's death, with the Healing Revival and Oral Roberts. Thousands of people were quickened by the Holy Spirit, and the Charismatic Revival had similar far-reaching effects on both individuals and established churches. Wigglesworth then saw that the supernatural manifestations were held back until an army of teachers appeared to train the body of Christ. That took place through the Faith Movement. Afterwards, all the power and revelation which the Lord had previously poured out would combine to cause the greatest revival in world history. The outpouring of the Spirit, symbolized by fall and spring rains, would descend and ripen the harvest—a harvest which would be reaped by supernaturally-equipped workers. Then the Lord would return.

> Be patient, then, brothers, until the Lord's coming. See how the farmer waits for the land to yield its valuable crop and how patient he is for the autumn and spring rains (Jas 5:7).

A mounting sense of expectation has been felt throughout the 20th century as the Church has anticipated the Lord's return. Everything must be restored and the Church Age complete before He arrives.

Ephesians 5:27 says that the Lord will place the Church before Him *to present her to himself as a radiant church, without stain or wrinkle or any other blemish, but holy and blameless.*

Before Jesus' return, the Church will come into that position. She will be cleansed from all worldliness, backsliding, impurity and weakness. She will be completely committed to Jesus, like a bride whose eyes search for her husband-to-be, glorious, beautiful, full of love and devotion.

> Arise, shine, for your light has come, and the glory of the Lord rises upon you. See, darkness covers the earth and thick darkness is over the peoples, but the Lord rises upon you and his glory appears over you (Isa 60:1,2).

The Lord is accelerating the restoration process to bring this promise to fruition. Therefore, the Church must prepare for three things:

1. To successfully deliver the gospel, in the power of the Holy Spirit, and bring in the last harvest of peoples from every tribe and nation before the Lord's return.

2. To reflect the glory of God as a strong, growing Church. Believers' lives should be totally committed to God, giving Him all the honor. This is vital for the future when evil will arise as never before.

3. To be prepared, motivated and mature, ready to be taken by Jesus on His return.

The third stage is rapidly taking place and it embraces many different areas, all of which concern service.

First, to *serve the world* in the power of the Spirit with the full gospel, for salvation, healing and deliverance.

Second, to *serve the Church,* the body of Christ, with life, strength, faith and revelation, so that the believer grows into full, Christ-like maturity (Eph 4:13).

Third, to *serve God* through a holy life-style—with praise, worship, love and appreciation—to give God all the honor He is worthy to receive.

In the future, we will see all these different stages of restoration coming together. This does not mean that all Christian associations or movements which were formed as a result of revelation will merge. But the Lord will take various revelations concerning His Church and bring them together. All human ideas or actions will not necessarily center on these truths—but the truths themselves will be joined as stones in God's structure, complementing one another perfectly.

The result will be a strong, victorious Church, whose solid foundation is revelation, truth and sound doctrine, and whose cornerstone is Jesus Christ. Her walls are built of born-again believers who live holy lives and become pillars in God's temple. Her roof is decorated with God's power, revelation and presence through the Holy Spirit's many-sided ministry. All this combines to create the dwelling-place in which God lives by His Spirit (Eph 2:20-22).

The Church will be restored, cleansed, prepared, devoted and filled with His presence. She will be well equipped to fulfill her purpose, and complete her assignment in victory before Jesus comes and the Church Age closes. This process of preparation and restoration will gain momentum. In the final phase everything will intensify, the glory will increase, and the result will be tremendous!

4

Five Pillars of the Vision

The vision and the assignment which the Lord gives the local church must be made clear. Whatever the Lord reveals, can be understood by man. God anoints His Word so that when people hear and receive it, they are assured success.

> Have faith in the Lord your God and you will be upheld; have faith in his prophets and you will be successful (2 Chron 20:20).

If individual members receive in their hearts God's prophetic Word to their church, then both the church and its members will prosper.

God wants the Church to be successful, and this is achieved through His Word.

> So the word of God spread. The number of disciples in Jerusalem increased rapidly (Acts 6:7).

A prerequisite for growth is God's Word, His spoken address, which must be received in faith.

The Church must also have a conviction that it is God's will for it to grow. It needs to commit itself to this idea, to believe it and stand firm in this belief. All life contains growth. The process may vary in time and appear to be otherwise—but it will come. Never let the devil rob you of your faith for growth!

The vision which the Lord gives the local church contains growth, so pillars are needed to support it. Five pillars must be established in the Church so that the vision—God's will for the Church—can be fulfilled. They are:

1. The preaching of the Word.
2. Praise and worship.

3. Prayer.
4. Evangelization.
5. Fellowship.

All these are necessary to create a strong, stable and balanced church.

The local church is the place for all believers. There is room for each one to grow and work. The Church is also the place for all revelation. The Lord often puts specific duties and particular revelations on believers' hearts but the place to receive, develop and practice these is within the local church. The Church is therefore broad because it encompasses so much. However, that does not mean it just accepts everything, with everyone going in different directions. No, it must go forwards, in one direction, yet be broad enough to allow for diversity. It is like a plough, which has a point at the front and a wide part at the back, while its weight bears downwards so that it breaks through the earth.

The First Pillar: PREACHING THE WORD

> They devoted themselves to the apostles' teaching and to the fellowship (Acts 2:42).

Every activity the Church undertakes must have its foundation in the Word. Only God's Word has the anointing to penetrate and change. When Paul left the local church at Ephesus, he said in Acts 20:32:

> Now I commit you to God and to the word of his grace, which can build you up and give you an inheritance among all those who are sanctified.

When he left, he entrusted them to God to continue building them up through His Word.

The Church grew as it was "watered" by the preaching of the Word. They *devoted themselves to the apostles' teaching and to the fellowship, to the breaking of bread and to prayer* (Acts 2:42). The apostles *were all filled with the Holy Spirit and spoke the word of God boldly* (Acts 4:31), and *the word of God spread. The number of disciples in Jerusalem increased rapidly* (Acts 6:7). When persecution began, the apostles scattered and *those who had been scattered preached the word wherever they went* (Acts 8:4).

Without the preaching of the Word, the world cannot be saved, and believers cannot be strengthened. Therefore Satan hates the Word and continually attacks it. The Word is the sword of the Spirit (Eph 6:17). Without the Word we cannot fight against Satan, and if he is given an opportunity to distort the gospel, he will use it.

There are two traps in which Satan would have us ensnared. First, there is the worldly, rationalistic denial of the Word, and many theological institutions have fallen into this. The other trap is to place personal experiences, revelations and feelings before the Word of God. God does not want to withhold revelations and visions, but they are always aligned with His Word and must be tested accordingly. Without this, we would waver and fall.

The Bible speaks about the supernatural. Therefore, Christians who affirm the Bible's credibility cannot also deny its supernatural aspect—healings, miracles and deliverance from demons. Take a positive attitude to the Bible and acknowledge the Spirit's supernatural intervention. Then you will recognize the genuine and distinguish it from the false. However, the devil is cunning enough to conjure his own supernatural manifestations which are not connected in any way with God's Spirit. But if someone is afraid of the supernatural he will not understand the gospel, and this will only hinder and grieve the Holy Spirit.

Paul says that he will not preach on anything *except what Christ has accomplished through me in leading the Gentiles to obey God by what I have said and done—by the power of signs and miracles, through the power of the Spirit. So from Jerusalem all the way around to Illyricum, I have fully proclaimed the gospel of Christ* (Rom 15:18,19). Wherever the Word was preached, it was supernaturally confirmed with signs and wonders:

> Then the disciples went out and preached everywhere, and the Lord worked with them and confirmed his word by the signs that accompanied it (Mark 16:20).

God's Word is normally followed by signs and wonders. There is nothing unusual or abnormal about this. This is normal Christianity according to the New Testament.

Whenever the Word is preached, God's Spirit is there to confirm it with signs and wonders. Some Christians are afraid of miracles and in disbelief they warn others about the working of the Holy Spirit. Yet there are others who have a fixation with signs and wonders. God has never intended that we should breeze through the preaching and then try to work up a show of miracles like a circus performance!

Above all, God wants to implant His Word in people's hearts where it will grow into answers to prayer, victory, revelation, guidance and miracles. The Holy Spirit longs to respond, on the basis of the Word, with powerful works and miracles in the believer's life!

Preach the Whole Counsel of God

When Paul preached to the church at Ephesus, he said in Acts 20:27:

> For I have not hesitated to proclaim to you the whole will of God.

This means that a church must receive all that God has revealed for it through the preaching, not just certain details, pet doctrines or specific revelations. So, when Paul speaks of the pastor, he says:

> He must hold firmly to the trustworthy message as it has been taught, so that he can encourage others by sound doctrine and refute those who oppose it (Tit 1:9).

Paul repeatedly emphasized the importance of preaching the gospel and the whole word of the Bible because *all Scripture is God-breathed and is useful for teaching, rebuking, correcting and training in righteousness, so that the man of God may be thoroughly equipped for every good work* (2 Tim 3:16,17).

The fundamental doctrines must be established in a believer's life. God's Word is *spirit and life* (John 6:63) and gives life, strength and victory to everyone who receives it.

> Consequently, faith comes from hearing the message, and the message is heard through the word of Christ (Rom 10:17).

Therefore, Jesus prays *for those who will believe in me through their message* (John 17:20).

We can never over-emphasize the importance of God's Word:

1. The Word is God (John 1:1).
2. The Word creates (Gen 1:1), and sustains creation (Heb 1:3).
3. The Word causes the new birth (1 Pet 1:23; Jas 1:18).
4. The Word is food for the inner man (Matt 4:4).
5. The Word is the sword of the Spirit (Eph 6:17; Rev 1:16; Matt 4:4,7,10).
6. The Word heals (Prov 3:8, 4:22; Ps 107:20; Matt 8:8,13).
7. The Word delivers (Matt 8:16).
8. The Word gives long life (Prov 3:2, 4:10,22, 9:11).
9. The Word brings peace (Prov 3:2).
10. The Word gives wisdom (Prov 2:1-6).
11. The Word gives protection (Ps 119:9).
12. The Word assures victory over sin (Ps 119:11).
13. The Word ensures success (Josh 1:8; Ps 1:1-3).
14. The Word gives participation in God's divine nature (2 Pet 1:4).
15. The Word provides everything which leads to life and holiness (2 Pet 1:3).

This list would be considerably lengthened if we were to note everything that God's Word is, has, and can accomplish. God's Word above all, concerns Christ, and Christ is the Word (John 1:1), who *became flesh and dwelt among us* (John 1:14, NKJV). Therefore, the preaching of the Word is the gospel—the good news about what God has done for every individual, in and through Jesus Christ. Above all, we should preach Christ and His full gospel.

The Full Gospel of Jesus

What is the gospel? Luke says in Acts 1:1 *In my former book* (Luke), *Theophilus, I wrote about all that Jesus began to do and to teach.* The gospel is *everything* that Jesus did, and *everything* He taught! If anyone subtracts anything from this, he is not preaching the *whole* gospel.

What did Jesus do?

> Jesus went through *all* the towns and villages, teaching in their synagogues, preaching the good news of the kingdom and healing *every* disease and sickness (Matt 9:35).

Jesus laid these foundations:
a) He preached and proclaimed the Kingdom of God.
b) He taught on the Kingdom of God.
c) He forgave sins.
d) He healed the sick.
e) He drove out evil spirits.

Everything He did was God's will and it was good news for all people. To evangelize is to preach the same things today, since Hebrews 13:8 says that *Jesus Christ is the same yesterday and today and forever.*

The gospel is also *everything* that Jesus did through His death. "He descended into hell, and on the third day rose from the dead. He ascended into heaven, and sits on the right hand of God Almighty," as described in one of the confessions of the Church. The gospel is Jesus' business here on earth, but above all, His reconciling, sacrificial death and resurrection. This allowed mankind to regain fellowship with God and live, in part, the godly life Jesus demonstrated here on earth.

All that Jesus did on the cross is best described in Paul's letters. It can be summarized as knowledge on:

1. What man is in Adam through the Fall.

2. What man is in Christ through salvation and restoration.

3. What Jesus did for us on the cross.

4. What the Holy Spirit does for us through the new birth.

5. What Jesus does for us through His intercession at the Father's right hand.

6. What the Holy Spirit does through us here on earth.

7. What God has prepared in heaven for those who believe.

This can be summarized as knowing:

1. Who God is, what He has, and what He can do.

2. Who you are, what you have and what you can do.

3. Who your enemy is, what he has, and what he can do.

God wants every believer to understand and live in the light of this knowledge. Paul prays for the believers *that the God of our Lord Jesus Christ, the glorious Father, may give you the Spirit of wisdom and revelation, so that you may know him better. I pray also that the eyes of your heart may be enlightened in order that you may know the hope to which he has called you, the riches of his glorious inheritance in the saints, and his incomparably great power for us who believe* (Eph 1:17-19).

It is vital that believers have a revelation of their identity and their authority in Christ. We must know what the Father did *for us* through Christ's sacrifice on the cross, through His death and resurrection. We must understand our present position *in* Christ Jesus. We must know the inheritance which *is* accessible to us, and *how* we can draw from it. We must know what we can do *in and through* Christ, not just for Him, but *in and through* Him. We should not be ignorant of our enemy as this would allow him advantage over us. *For we are not unaware of his schemes* (2 Cor 2:11). We must all recognize Satan's strategies, tactics and propaganda, and above all his crushing defeat and our victorious position in Christ over him (Eph 1:20-23).

All this can be summarized in the basic doctrines outlined in Hebrews 6:1,2:

> Therefore let us leave the elementary teachings about Christ and go on to maturity, not *laying* again the *foundation* of repentance from acts that lead to death.

These are the "elementary teachings":

1. **Repentance from dead works**—repentance, (the Greek is metánoia = change of mind).

2. Faith toward God—*The just shall live by faith* (Rom 1:17, NKJV).

3. *Doctrine of baptisms*:

a) The baptism in Christ—the new birth.

b) The baptism to Christ—water baptism.

c) The baptism of the Holy Spirit.

4. **Laying on of hands** (three types in the NT):

a) For healing and deliverance (Mark 16:18).

b) For the Spirit's baptism and gifts of grace (Acts 19:6, 8:17; 2 Tim 1:6).

c) For dedication to the ministry (Acts 13:3, 6:6).

5. **Resurrection of the dead**.

6. **Eternal judgment**.

The Holy Spirit wants to mediate all this to the believer, through the different ministerial gifts. This will *prepare God's people for works of service, so that the body of Christ may be built up* (Eph 4:12). Nothing is more important than building up the body of Christ so that believers will be strong overcomers who learn to live in personal victory. Then the Kingdom of God will really expand!

Receive the Word in your Heart

When the Word is preached and affirmed with signs and wonders, it must be received in the hearts of the hearers. Wherever the Word is preached, there are different hearts, different qualities of soil. When Jesus explained His parable of the sower in Mark 4:1-20, He spoke about the different kinds of responses to the Word in an individual's life.

The seed which is sown is the Word (Mark 4:14) and it has a guaranteed harvest. There is nothing wrong with the seed, but soil quality can differ. Therefore, the Word must be preached without compromise. The Word is both teaching (*didache*) and exhortation (*pareklesis*). Some people want only to be titillated so *they will gather around them a great number of teachers to say what their itching ears want to hear* (2 Tim 4:3).

Both teaching and exhortation are found in all Paul's letters. Without exhortation, the believer's life does not change, resulting in mere intellectual acceptance. There will be no deep conviction of the Spirit, which pierces even to the division of the soul and spirit and discerns the motives of the heart (Heb 4:12). When the Word is preached there are many different spiritual types among the listeners. Generally, they can be divided into two groups: the born-again, and those who are not born-again.

Among the born-again believers there are:

a) Those who want to follow Jesus with all their hearts on His conditions. They are sensitive in the spirit, have clean and tender hearts, and are teachable and open. They are not perfect, but they have victory, joy and freedom in their lives. They love Jesus and will gladly speak about Him.

b) The other category consists of those who want to follow the Lord on *their own* conditions. They are often "spiritual" and have many plans and ideas. But if things don't go their way, they are easily upset, discouraged, critical or angry. They want to serve the Lord with themselves in the center. As long as they stand in the spotlight where they can exert *their* will, it will be "hallelujah" all the way. But when the Lord's Spirit starts to work on them, they will either be broken and realize that their Christian life was built upon egotistic, fleshly motives, or otherwise their hearts will become hardened. Worldliness, rebellion and compromise remain in their lives. Hardness, apathy, superficiality, worldly pleasures and attitudes are still part of their personality. They do not want to be convicted by the Spirit in these areas and bring them to the cross. Hence, they defend similar behavior among other believers and win friends among other spiritually immature Christians. If they humbled themselves before the Word, the Spirit and the cross, they would receive a wonderful freedom and restoration in their lives. Should they refuse to humble themselves, rejection, hardening, rebellion and division will naturally follow. Then they will inevitably take offence, leaving God or the Church, with the accusation that *"this is a hard teaching"* (John 6:60). They forget that it is *the Spirit* (who) *gives life; the flesh counts for nothing* (John 6:63).

c) The third category consists of those who are born-again but have joined themselves with the world and given up the "good fight" to live in backslidden defeat. They are restless and weak, unhappy and miserable. They want to be in God's Kingdom, but the devil has convinced them that the cost is too high. They can never pay the price, and they will never overcome temptation or live in victory. At a time of temptation they failed, and they accepted Satan's lie that God does not love them anymore, the race is run and the gate is shut. Therefore, they feel uneasy at spiritual meetings. They feel exposed, backslidden and isolated and would rather flee from the presence of God. Yet when they are out in the world they do not find satisfaction there, either. In their hearts they long for God and do not want to sin. Hence, they are left out of worldly society, not being able to fit in there either. They are neither here nor there and are very uncomfortable. If they humbled themselves and came back to God, they would find a glorious restoration, and experience His love more than ever. But if they continue to flee, they will become hardened and embittered and give themselves completely over to the world. Then they will become one of the most hostile enemies of the gospel, since *it is impossible for those who have tasted the goodness of the word of God and the powers of the coming age, if they fall away, to be brought back to repentance* (Heb 6:5,6). No one can hate God like the person who has tasted His goodness and then rejected Him. No one lives an unhappier life.

Just as there are categories of born-again believers, there are different kinds of people who are not born-again:

a) The first is the normal heathen. He knows almost nothing about the gospel. He is dead in sin (Eph 2:1), but has never really made a conscious decision to reject God. He does not oppose the gospel, yet when revival comes and persecution for the Word's sake appears in the mass media, he is easily drawn into the current of negative propaganda. Nearly all his life he has depended on other people's ideas. His ideas are formed by the State, politics, and mass media. If he is not reached by the gospel and saved, his downfall will be that he never dared to think independently. He was always a coward, sensitive to peer pressure.

b) Then, there is the person who has felt the touch of the Holy Spirit and started to listen to the gospel. His conscience is pricked and he becomes sensitive to sin, righteousness and judgment (John 16:8-11). He begins to understand that he should change his ideas, perceptions and lifestyle. Once, he slept smugly in sin's false sense of security: "Everything will work out," "I'm only human," "I'm not worse than others," "If he exists, God will probably love me, so I won't have to worry." But now, through the Spirit's conviction, he starts to feel uneasy in his conscience. He regrets the sin in his life, but finds no way out. A few of these people will adopt the outward appearance of Christianity without coming to repentance from the heart. They go to church, do some good works, refrain from alcohol on Saturday nights, and give increasing amounts of money to some charity organization. This is good of course, but it does not save a lost soul or give peace with God.

A person must be born again (John 3:3). He must humble himself and accept the reality of Calvary, and the message of grace. If God's Spirit is allowed to continue to break through, he will eventually be saved and find peace with God. If he is content with his few, good religious deeds he will eventually become a religious opponent of true spiritual life. Alternatively, he may become bored and return to the world, but this time it will be harder than before, and he will be more difficult to reach again.

These different types are often represented at a meeting where the gospel is preached. God has a living word for each one, so that each individual can recognize his particular situation. Then he will see God's grace and find victory and freedom.

The Second Pillar: PRAISE AND WORSHIP

> Every day they continued to meet together in the temple courts. They broke bread in their homes and ate together with glad and sincere hearts (Acts 2:46).

Just as God speaks personally to His people through preaching from the Bible, with following signs and wonders, so His people can respond personally to Him through praise and worship. God wants His people to praise Him.

The believer's duty is to be a kingly priesthood. The kingly aspect advocates commanding, binding, loosing, and proclaiming the will of the Lord. The priestly aspect involves coming into the Lord's presence, partly for freedom in intercession, and partly for God's sake, to serve before Him.

In Acts 13:2 it says that *they were worshiping the Lord.* Worship is a service to the Lord. This means that they praised and blessed God, while speaking, singing and making music before His face. They expressed their love, joy, worship and enthusiasm for Him, showing how glorious, merciful and good He is.

Praise and Worship is Service Before God

God abides in the praises of His people. Great power, glory and revelation are released when God's people come with priestly service before His face.

My soul will boast in the Lord; let the afflicted hear and rejoice (Ps 34:2).

God wants to see our hearts continually humbled before Him, so that we can always praise and exalt Him.

Praise the Lord, all you servants of the Lord who minister by night in the house of the Lord (Ps 134:1).

When we bless the Lord, He can bless us *with every spiritual blessing in Christ* (Eph 1:3).

God loves our worship and praise, which is precious and holy to Him. We are His spiritual temple in this Church Age (Eph 2:21,22). He requires daily sacrifices, prayer and burning of incense, just as He did in the temple of the Old Testament. The sacrifice is that of praise; the incense comes from the prayers of holy people; and the worship comes from the priests, who are the believers. Therefore, Hebrews 13:15 says:

Through Jesus, therefore, let us *continually* offer to God a sacrifice of praise—the fruit of lips that confess his name.

The Devil Attacks Strong, Free Praise and Worship

When believers start to praise God, they perform a tremendously powerful service before God in the spirit realm. The devil wants to silence them, since worship in song is a force which God has laid in the mouths of babes and infants to defeat the avenger (Ps 8:3; Matt 21:16).

The enemy will do anything to stifle praise. He does not want you to *let the word of Christ dwell in you richly as you teach and admonish one another with all wisdom, and as you sing psalms, hymns and spiritual songs with gratitude in your hearts to God* (Col 3:16).

The devil hates hearing songs of praise here on earth. He wants to control the music to make it worldly and perverse. He also attacks believers through traditionalism, worldliness and sin, to smother strong and loud praise to the living God. There is often fear and contempt among

Christians for living and free worship. Why? Because when the Holy Spirit takes control of the music and God's glory is manifested, hidden sin in people's lives is exposed.

Praise and worship is a powerful tool encouraging:

1. God's presence in the congregation.
2. Conviction and cleansing in believers' lives.
3. An atmosphere for healing and revelation.
4. An advantage over Satan's influence and a change in the spiritual climate.

No wonder Satan hates the sound of praise! He does not want God to be honored and exalted, because he wants that for himself. Neither does he want people to be free. If he cannot bind them in worldliness, then he will try to bind them in unbiblical traditionalism and religiosity.

God wants believers set free to worship Him. Religion wants to restrain praise and worship, but God constantly speaks about sound:

> *Sing for joy* to God our strength; shout aloud to the God of Jacob! (Ps 81:1).

> *Shout for joy* to the Lord, all the earth. Serve the Lord with gladness; come before him with *joyful* songs (Ps 100:1,2).

> Let them praise his name with *dancing* and make music to him with tambourine and harp (Ps 149:3).

> *Clap your hands,* all you nations; shout to God with cries of joy (Ps 47:1).

God wants us to praise and worship Him with loud shouts, rejoicing and celebrating. He wants to see us full of joy, with uplifted hands, clapping and dancing! He wants to see enthusiasm, joy and intensity! Why? Because He is worthy of everything we have! Our bodies are *living sacrifices, holy and pleasing to God—which is your spiritual worship* (Rom 12:1), which brings the sacrifice of praise. Our limbs are weapons of righteousness which God uses in battle against the enemy (Rom 6:13,14).

Besides being a means of bringing honor to God and establishing His presence, praise is a weapon against the enemy.

> May the praise of God be in their mouths and a double-edged sword in their hands, to inflict vengeance on the nations and punishment on the peoples, to bind their kings with fetters, their nobles with shackles of iron (Ps 149:6-8).

Praise and Worship Changes the Spiritual Atmosphere

Praise and worship also has another effect. Hostile spiritual principalities and powers are bound, the activities of darkness are frustrated, and the devil's schemes are exposed, causing a change in the spiritual atmosphere. No wonder the enemy wants to bind God's people and block them from freely praising God in the Spirit!

First Corinthians 14:15 speaks about worship with the understanding and worship in the Spirit. When a believer is baptized in the Holy Spirit, tongues begin to flow out from within him. Tongues can flow out in different melodies so the believer can worship God musically as well. The Holy Spirit takes over and breaks all boundaries of language, expression and melody. Songs of worship then flow from the depths of the believer to the Highest.

God wants all believers to speak in tongues and sing in the Spirit. This gives a new dimension to worship which results in greater glory and praise to God. The believer's priestly service becomes holier and stronger. Jesus becomes the focus, not human ability, musical talent or taste. Praise and worship is not a performance but the expression of the heart's innermost being, enraptured in the wonder, glory and salvation of the most high God.

The Third Pillar: INTERCESSORY PRAYER

> So Peter was kept in prison, but the church was earnestly praying to God for him (Acts 12:5).

Everything God does in and through His Church comes as response to prayer. First, He places a task or a vision in the church's heart. This is followed by a spirit of intercessory prayer, whose labor brings the desired event to fruition. God answers prayer in this way, and growth, miracles, revival and breakthrough come. James says *you do not have, because you do not ask* (Jas 4:2). A church which neglects prayer will never see growth, much less expect to survive! Every revival has been birthed through prayer. Prayer develops sensitivity to God. Then believers can come into obedience and carry out His command.

When Paul instructs believers to put on the whole armor of God in order to stand on the day of evil, he says:

> And pray in the Spirit on all occasions with all kinds of prayers and requests. With this in mind, be alert and always keep on praying for all the saints (Eph 6:18).

The Church was birthed through prayer (Acts 1:14), grew through prayer (Acts 2:42), overcame opposition through prayer (Acts 4:24-31), had miracles through prayer (Acts 12:5) and consecrated ministries through prayer (Acts 13:3). Prayer is at the heart of the Church, and every member must have a spirit of prayer in his life.

Often, the pastor, the church leadership and a few specialists carry the whole burden of prayer for the church. Church prayer meetings have traditionally been the least attended of all, but that is no longer the case. Today, hundreds of people gather daily for prayer and that makes a vast difference in the spirit world.

There are many kinds of prayer: worship and praise, thanksgiving, prayers of commitment, intercession, personal prayer, prayers of authority, prayers of agreement, faith, and so on. The Holy Spirit will lead the Church into the appropriate type of prayer for a particular purpose.

The prayer life of a church is no stronger than the prayer lives of its individual members. When the believer realizes that all the resources and blessings of the Covenant are available through prayer, he will want to sharpen his prayer life. As long as a believer sees God as distant, angry or negative, prayer will be a drudge, yielding few results. But when the Holy Spirit is allowed to show how powerful and simple prayer is, all this will change.

God Responds to Prayer

Let us then approach the throne of grace *with confidence,* so that we may receive mercy and find grace to help us in our time of need (Heb 4:16).

Through His lovingkindness, God has made Himself accessible to us!

And without faith it is impossible to please God, because anyone who comes to him must believe that he exists and that *he rewards those who earnestly seek him* (Heb 11:6).

Whenever Jesus teaches on prayer in the New Testament, He emphasizes answered prayer and this is the purpose of prayer. God responds to prayer. Jesus said,

And I *will* do *whatever* you ask in my name, so that the Son may bring glory to the Father. You may ask me for *anything* in my name, and I *will* do *it* (John 14:13,14).

Jesus' words are perfectly clear: He sets no limit to what we can pray for (John 15:7,16; John 16:23,24; Matt 21:22; Jas 1:7,8; 1 John 5:14,15). Yet we limit God's willingness to answer our prayer. Jesus said,

In that day you will no longer ask me anything. I tell you the truth, my Father *will* give you whatever you ask in my name (John 16:23).

What an asset!

When a believer realizes what God has made available to him, and how willing He is to answer and do miracles, his prayer life will be completely transformed! God's willingness to respond to prayer is much greater than our willingness to pray.

We Pray From a Position of Authority

And God raised us up *with* Christ and seated us with him in the heavenly realms in Christ Jesus (Eph 2:6).

We are in Christ Jesus, placed in the kingdom of the beloved Son (Col 1:13). We are in Christ, high above all spiritual principalities and powers (Eph 1:20-23). We are God's beloved children (Eph 5:1). We have received a spirit of adoption whereby we cry *Abba Father* (Rom 8:15).

If God is for us, who can be against us? (Rom 8:31).

When we receive the revelation that God is a Father who is full of lovingkindness, then it will not be difficult to pray.

Jesus says:

If you, then, though you are evil, know how to give good gifts to your children, *how much more* will your Father in heaven *give good gifts* to those who ask him! (Matt 7:11).

The key to a successful prayer life is to realize the Father's goodness and willingness to give. Above all, see that exalted position of intimacy which the Father has bestowed on His children, placing them high above all opposition.

Authority in the Name of Jesus

Jesus says:

Until now you have not asked for anything *in my name*. Ask and you will receive, and your joy will be complete (John 16:24).

Revelation on the name of Jesus is vital. It is not merely the way we conclude our prayers, but the name which gives the prayer validity and secures an answer from God.

The name of Jesus represents His person, resources and capability. Since Jesus is God's Son, all the resources of heaven are available to Him. Jesus has paid the ransom for sin, defeated the devil and brought reconciliation through His blood. Therefore, His name is an essential requirement for salvation. When a believer uses His name in prayer, it represents everything that Jesus is, everything He has and all He has accomplished. This can be summarized in one word: salvation!

> Salvation is found in no one else, for there is no other name under heaven given to men by which we must be saved (Acts 4:12).

Three things happen when we use Jesus' name:

1. Heaven listens attentively. Jesus' name is valid there.

2. The powers of darkness shudder. Jesus' name means total victory over the enemy. He must flee before that name.

3. Circumstances change. God answers prayer in Jesus' name and miracles happen.

We can pray to the Father, command Satan and speak to circumstances in Jesus' name. Before a congregation can be strong in prayer, it must clearly understand God's willingness to answer prayer and know the believer's standing and authority in the name of Jesus. Then, led by the Spirit of God, the church can begin to pray. It will pull down strongholds, storm gates, crush resistance, bind, loose and stand in faith for answered prayer and miracles. God will respond and do the miraculous.

The Holy Spirit—Our Helper and Prayer Guide

The Holy Spirit's guidance is the most valuable asset we have for prayer. The Holy Spirit knows the Father's heart and will (1 Cor 2:10-12). He takes what is in the Father's heart and puts it in our hearts and helps us to pray it through.

> In the same way, the Spirit helps us in our weakness. We do not know what we ought to pray, but the Spirit himself intercedes for us with groans that words cannot express (Rom 8:26).

Sometimes we do not know how we should pray, but God's Spirit knows. Therefore, the Scriptures beseech us to *pray in the spirit*—pray in other tongues (1 Cor 14:15). Praying in other tongues is an invaluable resource which transcends the limitations of the intellect. God's Spirit can take what is in the Father's heart and bring it to fruition through the prayer of the believer who prays in the Spirit. Everything that God has given us in our church, Bible school and missionary work, has come through this type of prayer.

> And I will pour out on the house of David and the inhabitants of Jerusalem a spirit of grace and supplication. They will look on me, the one they have pierced, and they will mourn for him as one mourns for an only child, and grieve bitterly for him as one grieves for a firstborn son (Zech 12:10).

When the Holy Spirit comes over a believer, a prayer group or a church with a spirit of prayer, anything can happen. Once in 1980, a brother and I lay on the floor during a prayer meeting and sketched, from imagination, a map of Sweden. As we laid ourselves on top of it and started to pray, God's Spirit came over us strongly. Names of Swedish towns gushed forth within me as we prayed for revival in Sweden.

On another ocasion, praying in tongues gave way to deep sighing and groaning as God's Spirit came over our prayer group. I experienced my inner man going out over the earth and I found myself calling out nation after nation.

Once, during a summer conference at Eriksdalshallen, Stockholm, a spirit of prayer descended upon us on the platform. Praying in tongues gave way to sighing and loud cries. I experienced a heavy darkness coming over me which intensified as I lay on the platform before thousands of people. I started to feel hopelessness and misery, but I understood what it was. The Bible speaks about standing in the gap. I had been engulfed in the hopelessness unsaved people experience when they die and go to hell. After a moment of intercessory prayer, it lifted. Of course, people may think this is unusual, but the issue is not what the norm is, but what the Holy Spirit is doing.

The Lord can put special needs on intercessors' hearts which may be prayed through by tongues, inexpressible groans and cries. They are placed "in the gap" to travail and guard what God wants to do. This type of prayer has preceded every revival.

Another time when several of us were engaged in intercessory prayer, I felt the Lord's Spirit elevating me and my speech in tongues completely changed. I heard myself uttering a language which sounded Chinese. It happened quickly and in my inner man I felt the Spirit say: "Now you are praying for the different places, villages, and regions in China." It was a vivid experience and since then my heart has been intently preparing for China. At that time, the Lord's Spirit said: "One, two, three—Eastern Europe, Russia, China!" Since then we have seen our missionary work develop precisely that way.

The Holy Spirit knows much more than we do, and when we allow the spirit of prayer to come over us, we can undertake great exploits in the spirit and see the miraculous happen. Therefore, the local church must have a vigorous spirit of intercessory prayer.

The Fourth Pillar: EVANGELIZATION

Without evangelization, a church dies. A lake which has inflow without outflow will inevitably stagnate. God wants the Church to both receive and give. How wonderful newly-saved people are! They are the babies of the Church, but nothing is more refreshing to them than witnessing to the lost. Every believer has been saved to win others. Jesus said to His disciples: *"Come, follow me...and I will make you fishers of men"* (Matt 4:19).

The New Testament shows two kinds of evangelization, and Philip, the New Testament evangelist, practiced both mass evangelization and personal evangelization.

Evangelization means to proclaim the good news about Jesus in a way that is short, simple and easily understood.

Every believer can do this. You do not have to explain everything in the Bible or give an account of Church history. You are a witness, not the accused. Neither are you a prosecutor, nor a lawyer for the defence. As a witness, there are two basic things you should testify about. The first concerns the gospel.

> Then Philip began with that very passage of Scripture and told him the good news about Jesus (Acts 8:35).

Jesus is the focus of our discussion—who He is and what He has done. All evangelization, whether to the masses or to an individual, should include these simple, essential truths:

1. God loves the person and has a plan for his life (John 3:16).

2. Man, through sin, turned his back on God and became lost (Isa 53:6).

3. God sent Jesus for man's sake: to save and restore him (Rom 5:8).

4. One must receive God's invitation to salvation through faith (Eph 2:8,9; John 1:12).

All Can Understand
and Receive God's Invitation to Salvation

The gospel is simple and straightforward. All people in all countries and cultures can understand and receive God's invitation to salvation. Apart from background and culture, people are very much alike. There are certain basic needs and questions which all people have. God is both willing and able to answer these questions and meet these needs.

In ancient times, man sought his "destiny" or "fate" and this is still relevant in many cultures today. During Medieval times, "guilt and punishment" were important to the ordinary person. Now the current issue is finding "meaning." Many people are frantically trying to make something meaningful of their lives. But behind the cheerful facade, the restlessness and the pleasure-seeking, is a meaningless, empty void. God has the answer to futility, anguish and all desire to escape!

Common Questions—Biblical Answers

Many people have only a superficial knowledge of Jesus and the gospel. The questions they raise can be summarized in the following questions and statements:

1. *Isn't the Bible full of contradictions? Isn't it open to any favored interpretation?*

Answer: The Bible is not full of contradictions. Can you name any? (Most often people can't.) Of course there are difficulties. The Bible is not a superficial book, but its central message is completely clear and free from ambiguity. You cannot read the Bible whichever way you please. There are clear guidelines and principles of interpretation which must be applied in the same way to any piece of literature. Follow these guidelines, then it will be obvious what the Bible is saying. However, if words are plucked out of their respective contexts, then of course the meaning could be altered, but this is also true for any other book or message.

2. *How can a loving God condemn people to hell?*

Answer: God is full of love, but love cannot tolerate anything and everything. Love is based on truth. God is also a holy and just God. Justice demands that crime receives due punishment. No society can allow criminals to run free "out of love." There would be chaos! When people are lost, it is not God who is angry with them, it is they who have ignored Him. Man has a free will. God does not force anyone into heaven. When a person makes the decision to accept God or reject God, he has a free choice. Though God seeks the lost, the decision to choose Him is based on love, not on force.

> Whoever wishes, let him take the free gift of the water of life (Rev 22:17).

3. *How can you explain all the suffering in the world?*

Answer: Suffering cannot be explained apart from an understanding that there is a personal enemy to God and man: Satan. God gave the world to man to rule it. Man *chose* to sin. His dominion over creation was then immediately transferred to Satan who became *the god of this world* (2 Cor 4:4). 1 John 5:19 says: *The whole world is under the control of the evil one* and Jesus said that *The thief comes only to steal and kill and destroy; I have come that they may have life, and have it to the full* (John 10:10). God's solution to the problem of sin and suffering in the world is Jesus' victory on the cross and the whole gospel.

4. *What will happen to those who have never heard the gospel?*

Answer: God is completely righteous. He loves all people and He is totally just. No one will be able to say: "I never had the chance—you are unjust, God!" The Bible does not tell us what happens, but we can be sure that God is just. The issue is not what happens to those who have never heard, but what happens to those who have heard and yet refused!

5. *How can you account for all the miracles in the Bible?*

Answer: If God exists and He is almighty, then there is nothing remarkable about His performing miracles. As Almighty God, He can do whatever He wants. Some people say "I don't believe that Jesus walked on water." But if Jesus is God's Son—God in the flesh, why should it be inconceivable that He should walk on that lake, in that country, in that continent, in that planet which He himself had created and sustained with His Word? Miracles are only a problem if one does not account for God.

6. *Why is Church history so full of misery?*

Answer: Church history and biblical revelation are two different things. The Bible partly speaks about people who, despite being believers, walk in the flesh and consequently do wrong things. The Bible also says that we do not have to walk in the flesh.

> Therefore, brothers, we have an obligation—but it is not to the sinful nature, to live according to it. For if you live according to the sinful nature, you will die; but if by the Spirit you put to death the misdeeds of the body, you will live (Rom 8:12,13).

When believers choose not to follow Jesus, due to sin and rebellion in their lives, the result will be negative. Much has been done in Christianity and Jesus' name which has nothing to do with biblical Christianity, for example, the Crusades and persecution of the Jews. Much of this wickedness, which was committed in the Church's name, was caused by religious zealots who were neither born-again nor had Jesus as their role model. They were not led by God's Spirit, but were driven by another spirit. All this will be judged by God. Nevertheless, you cannot hide behind the Church's mistakes. You must personally consider what Jesus is saying to you through the gospel.

7. God doesn't exist. Everything is relative!

Answer: No one can conclude that God does not exist! No one has been able to produce any evidence to support such an unintelligent claim. On the other hand, a person can say that he doesn't know. Then he can begin to seek, and he who seeks finds! Jesus says:

> If any one *chooses* to do God's will, he *will* find out whether my teaching comes from God or whether I speak on my own (John 7:17).

In other words, if a person really *wants* to, he can have certainty of both God's existence and His will. An oft-heard statement is that "everything is relative." This is easy to say, but impossible to live by. Relativism would justify living a totally capricious, unethical, and undisciplined life: stealing may be wrong for me, but it may be right for you. It is only an attempt to sidestep the fact that

God has put in His Word and in people's consciences an indisputable, objective guideline by which they can live. Furthermore, its rationale backfires: is the exposition itself relative, or is it at the same time objective?

8. *Jesus was a good man who founded a religion, but He was not the only begotten Son of God.*

Answer: When people say Jesus was a religious pioneer, they usually mean it in a positive way, implying that He was a good man—but not the Son of God. That, however, is incomplete. A good man speaks truth. Jesus made great claims: He did not merely say He had the truth, but that He *was* the Truth. If what He claimed was false, then He was not a good man but a deceiver and he should be exposed as a deceiver and scoundrel. On the contrary, should His words be true, then people must take His claims seriously and pay attention to them. Many people say Christianity is intolerant, but if one way is right, then the other ways are wrong. This is not judgmental and narrow-minded, but a practical help for people to find life. Jesus said:

> "I am the way and the truth and the life. *No one* comes to the Father except through me" (John 14:6).

These are the most common objections people will raise. Some only wish to debate and are most probably not interested in the answer. For some, these intellectual speculations are the questions the Holy Spirit puts to them in their lives. Behind these questions, though, there is often a particular behavioral pattern which the person will not change. Instead of allowing the Holy Spirit to judge his morals or lack thereof, he dodges behind "intellectual doubt," clinging to a refusal to change his life-style.

For others these are genuine enquiries, since their hearts search for peace with God. When such a person hears a presentation of Jesus, he is less likely to respond with superficial speculations on, for example, "Adam's navel." First, give the biblical description of the gospel, then the Spirit can begin to work.

The Personal Witness

The second way to evangelize is by giving your personal testimony. Acts 4:20 says: *For we cannot help speaking about what we have seen and heard.* Share everything God has done in your life, all that Jesus has changed and what that means for you now. This is an effective witness for people around us today. Many people are longing for God to answer their prayer. When you tell of your answered prayer and the joy and fulfilment you have in God, it will penetrate their hearts.

When the disciples witnessed, the Holy Spirit was with them and He did wonders. When Jesus spoke to the woman at the well at Sychar (John 4), He received supernatural knowledge of her life. She was so convinced, that she told the whole town, and they believed when they heard and saw her.

> Many of the Samaritans from that town believed in him because of the woman's testimony, "He told me everything I ever did" (John 4:39).

You have the same Spirit and the same revelation in your life. He knows what goes on inside a person. I have often experienced how God's Spirit revealed thoughts, ideas and images which completely shattered all disbelief when an individual's personal situation was accurately described.

Once I witnessed to a Swede whom I met in Kathmandhu, Nepal. At first he was negative. Then I received a word from the Lord that he had lain sick in bed and cried out to God. When I told him that, his heart completely softened. He had recently been sick in Bangkok and thought that he would die. God knows what people do and think and what their situation is.

In the local church it is a known fact that ten percent of the members do ninety percent of the witnessing. And it is the newly saved who comprise most of this ten percent. Many begin to grow cool a few years after salvation. They lose their contacts and become cautious, or they separate themselves from the world, hiding behind the walls of a church. That is not God's will.

Every believer has a circle of contacts: relatives, friends and colleagues with whom he works or studies. This is his "Jerusalem," and he is empowered to witness there (Acts 1:8). If everyone had a burden to witness to his nearest acquaintances and won a few each year, a huge multiplication chain would begin. Therefore, the enemy tries to make believers fall asleep through intimidation, apathy or excuses such as "I'm so busy," for in that way other souls will slide into hell.

When believers are alerted to the seriousness and the responsibility of witnessing they will be glad to do so, and will experience the Holy Spirit's leading, power and wisdom. They will become fervent soul winners and save many people from wasteful lives. Evangelization will become the believer's life-style, and will motivate everyone to see the fruit of their work. This will be more than just a program or an activity, because it creates the basis for the Church's continuous growth.

> And the Lord added to their number daily those who were being saved (Acts 2:47).

A believer's foremost duty and privilege is to present the gospel, which is God's power for salvation, to the people he is with each day. There, he has contacts and opportunities which no other ministerial gift has. Therefore, the revival of the Last Days will be borne by strong believers who flow in their calling and in the power of the Holy Spirit. They will reach out to the modern world as never before.

The Fifth Pillar: FELLOWSHIP

When a person has received salvation, he is grafted into the body of Christ and placed beside other limbs. Life flows through the body, from one limb to another, from one cell to another. No one lives entirely for himself. When we were in the world, we were a poor and needy people, and sin made us completely self-centered. There is an unholy trinity called "I, me and mine." But through salvation and restoration, God meets our every need with His life, the abundant life. Therefore, God wants the believer to look to Him for all his resources.

God Wants to Fulfill Our Needs through the Church

When God created man and woman He created them with needs, but it was intended that He and no other would fill those needs. When the world, the flesh and the devil try to fill the needs, a person will only be hurt, disappointed and even demoralized. Sometimes, Christianity has ignored or denied the needs that people have, and even considered that position to be spiritual. But true spirituality allows God to fill these needs out of His goodness!

Man has spiritual, soulish, physical, social and financial needs. God does not limit Himself to one area, but wants to show His goodness and ability to perform wonders in *all* these areas. There is no part of human life where God will not touch people, meet their needs and build up His Kingdom!

Everyone has:

1. A need for security: to feel safe, at home, and in their right place.

2. A need for love: to be appreciated and accepted.

3. A need to rest: to have peace and harmony.

4. A need for change: to experience the new and interesting.

5. A need to succeed: to achieve something with which they are satisfied.

6. A need for the aesthetic: we are all drawn to beauty. God has nothing against this. He has created us in this way. But when a need drives and enslaves a person to

idolize it or seek salvation through it, it will destroy him.
God knows the desires of every heart:

> Delight yourself in the Lord and he will give you the desires
> of your heart (Ps 37:4).

There are not only "spiritual" needs in a church. Man is
also a social being. If *one* area alone is emphasized, that
will eventually result in an imbalance which only aggra-
vates problems. But through the Holy Spirit, a church
can meet all these needs. This does not imply that it
should be a type of social welfare institution, or long-term
rehabilitation clinic where people can expect to be coddled
all their lives, and where they can blame others for
becoming victims of "spiritual maltreatment."

Meet Other People's Needs

Every member is valuable to the church. They are not
just "cogs in a machine," helping to fulfill a vision, but
they are precious because God loves them and wants to
meet their every need. Zephaniah 3:17 reveals what God
thinks about every believer:

> The Lord your God is with you, he is mighty to save. He will
> take great delight in you, he will quiet you with his love, he
> will rejoice over you with singing.

This is God's attitude toward you! He loves you, He
rejoices and delights in you! He wants everything to be
well with you and wants to share increasingly more of
His life with you. You are totally accepted by Him, and
your place is in the local church. When a believer realizes
and accepts this fact, he will live in it. Then, he will be
freed *from himself* and begin to live for others. Since God
meets his needs so that his *cup overflows* (Ps 23:5), the
abundance of his life can overflow into others!

When a person surrenders his life to Jesus, his inner
needs are satisfied through Jesus' love. He experiences
God's lovingkindness and discovers His supernatural
ability to do miracles and meet all his life's needs. Living

with Jesus is exciting and full of joy. When a believer rolls all his troubles onto the Lord, in faith, and sees His support (1 Pet 5:7), he will be freed from himself to care for others. Through God's supernatural life, every believer can meet the needs of others each day.

Church members are not only there to "consume" the preaching. They can have fellowship with each other every day. Acts 2:46 tells us that the disciples met daily at two places: in the sanctuary and at home. This means that we find our identity through the Church. We do not merely "go to church." We *are* the church. It is as natural to be involved in the daily activities at the church building as it is to gather each day in private homes to pray, flow in the gifts, and help each other.

A person who merely contributes his presence to the church once or twice a week is barely with the church, but is more like an observer. God wants us to have our total identity and delight in loving and serving Jesus through the Church. Like a family unit, we can find rest, security and happiness there. This is not a place we visit, but a place we go out from and return to.

Cell Groups Strengthen Fellowship

The bigger a church, the greater its membership. Some fear that the church may also grow more impersonal, but it need never happen if a church has cell groups. Cell groups are just what the name implies: a cell in the body of the church. There, ten to twelve disciples meet and read the Word, share their needs, pray for each other, flow in the gifts and have fellowship with one another.

In large congregations—when everyone is assembled— it is impossible for everyone to share and prophesy. There is also a need for the various members to develop in their respective spiritual gifts, to care for one another and grow in knowledge. The place for that is within the cell group.

What then shall we say, brothers? When you come together, *everyone* has a hymn, or a word of instruction, a revelation, a tongue or an interpretation. All of these must be done for the strengthening of the church (1 Cor 14:26).

Each person can find his place in the cell group. He can feel welcome, at ease, open up and grow. He can also help in meeting the practical needs of others. Not least, the cell group is also a means for spreading the gospel through the one-to-one approach. Many people who are wary of going to a church meeting can meet cell group members in a private home. They can get to know believers in a natural way and so hear about Jesus.

The cell group is not an alternative to the church, but a natural extension of the church's life during the week. The believer who avoids these gatherings is open to isolation and serious problems.

> And let us consider how we may spur one another on toward love and good deeds. Let us not give up meeting together, as some are in the habit of doing, but let us encourage one another—and all the more as you see the Day approaching (Heb 10:24,25).

Basic teaching on faith should be repeatedly reinforced in the cell group. Someone may have heard the preaching on faith the Sunday before, but that is no guarantee that he has grasped everything. In the cell group he comes face to face with reality and the teaching should therefore be practical. Moreover, the cell group is the place where the teaching on the church vision is carried out. Then, everyone moves in one direction, instead of a thousand different directions. Through cell groups, each member can feel valuable and enjoy close fellowship with others, no matter how large the church becomes.

5

Church Leadership

A great deal has been written about Church leadership. Sometimes leadership has been over-emphasized so that everything else has been brushed aside. Such an imbalance will cause a church or movement to stagnate. When leadership becomes the overruling issue, wrong motives are usually at the helm. Then the situation will quickly lead to authoritativeness and power struggles.

Leadership is necessary. Without it there would be chaos. But it should serve the people and never be used as a platform for self-aggrandizement and control.

There are two snares we should avoid in the Church: pronounced collective leadership, and pronounced individual leadership. We risk falling into either of these when we use a single Bible verse to justify adopting one method or the other. A wrong understanding of Church leadership can restrict growth and life in a church.

Supporters of pronounced collective leadership are eager to use Bible terms such as "elders" and "councils of the apostles" pointing out that several persons made up the leadership of the Early Church. However, supporters of pronounced individual leadership use Galatians 1:16:

> To reveal his Son in me so that I might preach him among the Gentiles, I did not consult any man.

Both aspects of leadership contain some truth, but each view is correct only when balanced with the other. As a social being, man is both gregarious and individual and has respective needs in both categories. If we are to understand this fully, we must first sift out any secular thinking. Natural, soulish thinking stems from the carnal mind, and often sees leadership in a purely superficial way.

The issue of leadership often evokes negative reactions. Such thinking is motivated by fear of extremes and abuse of power. Instead of trying to understand what leadership entails and what God's thoughts are on the delegation of authority, they are driven by fear and disbelief. But beginning in the negative will never lead to the positive. Therefore, a revelation about leadership is vital.

Leadership is good. It has been placed in creation by God and He uses it to deal with man's needs and problems.

Man is Created to Have Dominion and Leadership

When God created man, He gave him authority to have dominion *over* creation.

> God blessed them and said to them, "Be fruitful and increase in number; fill the earth and *subdue it. Rule* over the fish of the sea and the birds of the air and over every living creature that moves on the ground" (Gen 1:28).

In the same way that God made fish to swim and birds to fly, He created man and gave him authority to have dominion over the earth. This has been inherent in man since creation; he is created for dominion and leadership (Gen 26-28).

Through the Fall, this mandate was perverted, misused and caused misery. Sin and selfishness led to the abuse of authority, power struggles, envy and rivalry. Yet the fact that the enemy took this ability and twisted it to suit his purposes, does not mean that we should ignore it or be ashamed of it. Leadership should be cleansed in Jesus' blood, consecrated for service in God's Kingdom, anointed by the Holy Spirit and used correctly. To shy away from leadership, or refuse it for fear of possible abuse or wrong influences, is no solution when faced with problems. Instead, we must sanctify and restore leadership so that it can be all that God intended.

First, we need to understand the purpose of leadership. We should not begin with questions on eldership for example, but with questions regarding the aim of leadership.

Leadership is Delegated Authority

Leadership is not a platform for power, but an appointment of delegated authority. Spiritual leadership does not function independently of God, but only through dependence on Him. God gives grace for leadership so that His children may be served.

> Who then is the faithful and wise servant, whom the master has put in charge of the servants in his household to give them their food at the proper time? (Matt 24:45).

Outlining a spiritual leader's role, we see that:

First: He is a subordinate to his Lord and has received his authority from Him, alone. He cannot take it upon himself.

Second: He is a servant, not a king.

Third: He is *not* an assistant. A position of authority is a position of oversight, supervision and leadership.

Fourth: His primary function is to minister to the people, not to gain privileges.

Leadership is found in all levels of human life: in social structures, politics, workplaces, in the family and in the Church. Denial, distortion or ignorance of leadership nurture chaos, confusion and anarchy. Furthermore, they leave an opening for the devil to come in to steal, kill and destroy.

Leadership entails aptitude and willingness to take responsibility. When people do not want to take responsibility, they often create structures where many, or really no one, decides. No single individual stands responsible in the end! But that is not God's way. We are all responsible before Him and we must all individually answer for our actions. Without accepting responsibility you can never become the person God has created you to be.

Leadership Begins with a Vision from God

Leadership always begins after God assigns a vision or a mandate to an individual. God spoke to Noah, Abraham, Moses, Joshua and David. Each received a specific mandate, a position of leadership and an anointing for the allotted task.

Ephesians 4:11 tells us that God *gave some to be...* and First Corinthians 12:28 says, *And in the church God has appointed...* God takes the initiative in delegating spiritual leadership. He calls, anoints and places a leader in the church. No individual can take it upon himself. Therefore, it is quite puzzling to see some people develop frustrations and fixations over their ministry. They are always wondering what their calling is, and whether others understand and recognize it. A person who is called to leadership need never strive and struggle to come into his calling, or seek opportunities or demand recognition of his ministry. All that is necessary is his willingness to serve others, his commitment in giving to others and working for their good. When he does that, God will select, anoint and appoint.

The mandate and the mission are more important than the ministry or the anointing. First, there is the mandate issued from heaven, then the ministry and finally the anointing. Unfortunately, many people focus entirely on the anointing. They rely on experiences, revelations and miracles to provide confirmation that they have been called and anointed. Don't do that! Keep the mandate and the vision in the center. Be like Issachar:

> Issachar is a rawboned donkey lying down between two saddlebags. When he sees how good is his resting place and how pleasant is his land, he will bend his shoulder to the burden and submit to forced labor (Gen 49:14,15).

First: Issachar found peace in his life.

Second: He accepted the task and went to work. This is what many church members need to do. First, they should find their place in Christ and learn to live and enjoy their inner life with God. Then they can start to work in the church, not out of frustration, ambition, a competitive spirit or religious duty, but out of joy, thankfulness and satisfaction.

A Leader Must Dare to Delegate

The Church is like a pleasant garden where people find peace, rest, security and fulfilment. But it is also a place where thousands of workers have found their place and work under the same vision and mandate. Finally, it is also an army where all are trained, developed and sent out to battle victoriously against the enemy.

When God gives a church a mandate, He also places a vision and a mission on the heart of the shepherd. This becomes very precious to him. At first, he is so preoccupied with it he thinks he has to do it all by himself. But the more it unfolds, he realizes that he lacks the capacity to handle all the details by himself. Therefore, he must delegate.

Moses found himself in this situation. He said:

> I cannot carry all these people by myself; the burden is too heavy for me (Num 11:14).

When God assigns a massive task to a servant there will come a point when it is impossible for him to continue unassisted. This is an important stage, because a spiritual feat can never be achieved through the flesh. When one arrives at that point, spiritual delegation becomes necessary. God placed the same spirit, the same anointing and the same mandate on seventy men so that *they will help you carry the burden of the people so that you will not have to carry it alone* (v 17). When the anointing came over these seventy elders, it did not mean that Moses abdicated, but instead, his ministry expanded. What God had given to Moses was furthered in and through the seventy men who would *help* him.

Once, in David's life several capable soldiers came over to him. He did not receive them all with open arms but said:

> If you have come to me in peace, to help me, I am ready to have you unite with me. But if you have come to betray me to my enemies when my hands are free from violence, may the God of our fathers see it and judge you (1 Chron 12:17,18).

When God assigns a mission to a servant He will also stand by him. This does not imply that the servant is perfect or mature. It means that God has given him a mandate, a mandate that is honored by Him. The church builds upon that word and that vision. Those who would be helpers must accept this, submit themselves and heed the call. Then the anointing will come over the vision and the person who carries that vision. This anointing will also come over those who help and work together for the fulfilment of the vision.

This does *not* imply that they should never question or talk about the vision, or discuss how it should be carried out. Some leaders have been so possessive about their call or vision that they never allow anyone to question anything about it or share in making decisions. After a while, it becomes very unsound and almost exclusive. The person who receives the vision will not necessarily always know *how* it should be undertaken. If you are blessed with good, loyal coworkers who are not seeking to take over, control or betray, then God will give them good ideas. Then they can help strengthen and develop the work in the right way.

Consider Moses. He made the classic mistake of doing everything by himself. People came to him for guidance and he sat alone from morning to evening, counseling an endless stream of Israelites who had every conceivable problem. His father-in-law, Jethro, saw this and said to him: *What you are doing is not good* (Ex 18:17). In other words, although the mission and the anointing are clear, the method can nevertheless be wrong.

> You and these people who come to you will only wear yourselves out. The work is too heavy for you; you cannot handle it alone (Ex 18:18).

We find the same principle operating here. God has issued a mandate, a mission and a vision to a spiritual leader, but it does not mean that he alone should carry out the entire task. He needs spiritual, mature, liberated, loyal and anointed coworkers! Nothing is more wonderful or more enjoyable than having a team of loyal coworkers. There is a balance here between individual and collective leadership. Note the balance in what Paul says in Galatians 1:16:

> To reveal his Son in me so that I might preach him among the Gentiles, I did not consult any man.

And see what we find in Proverbs 24:6:

> For waging war you need guidance, and for victory many advisers.

Paul—a Strong Leader with Many Coworkers

Paul is a good example of this. He is clear and secure in his calling. He speaks about himself and his ministry in a forthright way:

> Paul, an apostle—sent not from men nor by man, but by Jesus Christ and God the Father, who raised him from the dead—and all the brothers with me (Gal 1:1).

Paul is accompanied by coworkers and he refers to them by name:

> Paul, Silas and Timothy, To the church of the Thessalonians in God the Father and the Lord Jesus in Christ: Grace and peace to you (1 Thess 1:1).

He surrounded himself with a team who worked with him:

> He was accompanied by Sopater son of Pyrrhus from Berea, Aristarchus and Secundus from Thessalonica, Gaius from Derbe, Timothy also, and from the province of Asia Tychicus and Trophimus (Acts 20:4).

These were men of the same heart, vision and thinking as Paul. They flowed in unison toward a common goal. Each had his special task with his individual authority and integrity, yet all accepted Paul as the leader. When Paul received a vision, the team said:

> After *Paul* had seen the vision, we got ready at once to leave for Macedonia, *concluding* that God had called us to preach the gospel to them (Acts 16:10).

Paul's coworkers had freedom, but they did not have the liberty to do anything they pleased, however and whenever they liked. They all stood together under the same mandate which had to be carried out in a certain way, and God gave Paul complete oversight of the task.

As Paul said:

> The reason I left you in Crete was that you might straighten out what was left unfinished and appoint elders in every town, *as I directed you* (Tit 1:5).

Strong Leadership Does Not Limit Other Ministries Within the Church

All great work depends on strong leadership. But the leadership must be united under the same mandate. Without this, a few dominating individuals would pull the work in different directions through the flesh, causing jealousy and instability. Such people seek recognition for themselves and want to build their own platform from which they can compete to win the central position.

The pastor must be able to deal with this. But he cannot afford to react out of fear and suspicion. He must feel so secure in his calling that he does not feel threatened by another's initiative. He must dare to allow other gifts to emerge, and dare to train and correct them.

Those who work under a leader, for example a pastor, cannot do as they please. Yet no matter how strong a gift may be, it can grow and reach its full potential while functioning under another person's leadership, within the local church.

Evangelists and prophets have often thought that they cannot be rooted in a local church, as if it would limit their ministry in some way. Although their experience in other churches might have proved the case, it is nevertheless wrong. God wants every strong ministry to flow in, work through and stem from a strong local church.

The Leader's Duty is to Form the Coworkers

Coworkers are a necessity and good ones are worth more than gold. Therefore, they should be treated as such. They must be encouraged and know that they are valuable. They often do an enormous amount of work, so they are worthy of honor and thanks. When Moses had problems, his father-in-law, Jethro, helped him to analyze, define and assign the tasks which were needed (Ex 18:19-23).

Moses' work was then to:

a) Be the advocate and intercessor for the people before God (v 15).

b) Instruct them on the laws and statutes (v 20), in other words to preach the Word to them.

c) Show them which way they should go (v 20). Prophetically preach the way for the congregation and guide them in the right paths.

d) Show them what they should do (v 20). He had to define the people's tasks, show them that all are coworkers, and establish them in their different duties.

These are the pastor's duties:

1. The Word
2. Prayer
3. Prophetic leading
4. Work leader.

Everyone should hear from heaven and go in the same direction. Each person will then enter his respective calling and share his gifts. All are coworkers and soldiers marching in God's army. This is the Church's goal and it releases immeasurable energy. More is accomplished in this way than could ever be possible through a single ministry.

This is God's plan for the local church. He wants it to be a mighty institution for demolishing barriers, establishing truths, spreading the gospel, seeing God's power and expanding His kingdom. A united and goal-oriented church will no doubt invoke the wrath of Satan, but if it is built in the right way, then the gates of hell cannot withstand it.

Qualifications of a Good Coworker

After Moses had his particular work clarified, he received advice regarding his coworkers:

> But select capable men from all the people—men who fear God, trustworthy men who hate dishonest gain—and appoint them as officials over thousands, hundreds, fifties and tens. Have them serve as judges for the people at *all* times, but have them bring every difficult case to you; the simple cases they can decide themselves. That will make your load lighter, because they will share it *with you* (Ex 18:21,22).

Here we see that Moses seeks and chooses coworkers. No one chooses or assumes a position for himself.

The book of Proverbs says:

> Like an archer who wounds at random is he who hires a fool or any passer-by (Prov 26:10).

Do the work yourself until you find someone who is more apt. Do not start a project and then try to find someone to lead it. Instead, find someone who has a particular vision and anointing and then build the work around that.

All too often pastors have been in a hurry to establish their work. They think they must have Sunday School, day-care and evangelization all at once. They employ the first person who comes along and everything goes wrong. Find the right person first and then build. Then, the work will be sturdy and stable. Therefore, it is vital that coworkers are *"capable men who fear God, reliable men who hate dishonest gain."* There are four indispensable qualities which must be found in a coworker. He must be:

1. *God fearing.* We need to have faith in God, but we also need to have reverence for His every word, His methods, His presence and His will. When coworkers lose their respect for the Word, prayer, anointing or vision, problems will automatically arise. The standard of the work will sink, and it will resemble a secular organization more than a spiritual revival.

2. *Capable.* A person must be qualified. It is wonderful that employees have strong spiritual lives, pray in tongues and hear from heaven. However, they must also have practical skills for computer work, typewriting, accounting, organizing and so on. Believe God for productive people, otherwise the work will be hindered. If you must choose between an efficient, unsaved worker or one who is spiritual but inexperienced, choose the latter. However, it may not be necessary to make that choice if you believe God instead for spiritual people who are also very efficient!

3. *Reliable.* A pastor needs staff he can depend upon. They need not be completely mature, but they must be trustworthy. Dependability is a quality which causes a servant to receive God's favor and blessing.

Someone who serves a shepherd while also devising his selfish plans to further his own ministry, has a wrong spirit—that of selfish opportunism. This spirit came upon Gehazi, Elisha's servant, prompting him to swindle Naaman's wealth which Elisha declined to accept. Faithlessness, which is really absolute loyalty to oneself, is dangerous.

Faithless people serve and are dependable as long as it is expedient for them. They serve their own interests first, and when it no longer suits their plans or ambitions, they turn away despite any commitment they made. Such people use criticism to veil their own selfish motives. Faithlessness in people often appears when events "don't turn out the way they expected." Then it is obvious that egocentric, status-seeking ambitions motivated their service instead of a heart of service for the people. Ananias and Sapphira lived dishonestly and their dishonesty was exposed. They met death because their divided hearts would have spread the yeast of faithlessness throughout the Church. Therefore, it is essential that workmen are genuine, open and reliable believers.

4. *Hate dishonest gain.* This is a wonderful quality. Such people would never dream of taking financial advantages for themselves through the position they hold. They realize that favor, love and contacts have come their way through the church's ministry, not because they themselves are so remarkable. They do not draw personal, carnal favors from their contacts or their position. They are neither wasteful nor idle and do not misuse the funds which pass through their departments or area of responsibility. They are thorough, scrupulous and free in their relation to money. They would never imagine that *"godliness is a means to financial gain"* (1 Tim 6:5).

But "hating dishonest gain" is not restricted to money— it also applies to power and position. God gives a servant a position, to serve better and not to be a "mini pope." But if someone is not free in his spiritual life, he can be a target for worldly, carnal and demonic temptation. Some people completely change when they gain a senior position. They are no longer servants but power-mad dictators or primadonnas.

> Under three things the earth trembles, under four it cannot bear up: a servant who becomes king, a fool who is full of food, an unloved woman who is married, and a maidservant who displaces her mistress (Prov 30:21-23).

When such a person gets a position of authority and responsibility, he is not able to handle it with grace. The spiritual bondage in his life becomes apparent, making him oppress, hate and dominate people around himself. A whole work area can be oppressed because the leader himself is not free. On the other hand, it is equally destructive when a person in a subordinate position starts to show contempt and disregard for his boss. Such a person thinks "I am more anointed than the leader, I could do better." Then, the enemy sows disdain, rebellion and disharmony into his thoughts. Usually, he does not understand that God appoints positions, not only spiritual gifts. God has placed certain people in certain positions and He honors His decision.

Hagar scorned Sarah because she was infertile. The servant woman wanted to push aside her mistress. God did not like that and He dealt with Hagar. God honored Sarah's position although she could not conceive at the time.

To hate dishonest gain means to be scrupulous in one's motives, not straining for power and influence, and to be mindful of the limits of one's authority. It means to have an obliging, accommodating attitude, and one that is not self-seeking—whether in regard to finances, position, influence or attention. A coworker is a servant of God. Through faith in Him, he can work quietly while cultivating his spiritual life, walking in faith and trusting God to reward him.

6

Church Finance

All growth costs money. The greater the growth, the greater the need. The greater the need, the greater the increase in activity. This generates an increasing need for premises, and ever more employees are necessary. God wants every member of the Church actively involved in the work. There may be volunteers, but beyond this there is a need to employ workers. Both premises and employees cost money. As revival gains momentum, the work will grow and there will be an increasing financial need.

The Lord has imparted revelation on financial abundance and true biblical economy because there is such a tremendous need for money to finance revival and church growth. Therefore, it is tragic to see believers resisting this teaching. They do not understand that they saw off an arm which would deliver salvation and healing to thousands of people.

God Finances His Projects

God is a God of abundance. He is rich, almighty and good. He is a God who can finance all the projects which He initiates. He wants every church to be financially sound, strong and independent. Pastors and leaders must therefore be clear, pure and brave in the area of finances. They need to lead their churches into economic freedom. They need an uninhibited, bold spirit for the projects that the Lord puts on their hearts.

First, the pastor and his coworkers must develop faith for finances in their personal lives. Too many pastors have been over-cautious and stingy in their personal lives, reacting like the heathen out of worldly reckoning and fear, only to be constantly defeated. Their attitude then spreads over into the church, so that everyone is affected by this poverty-mindedness.

But when God's Word renews the leaders' thinking, victories are won on the personal level. Then God can use them and they can believe for the necessary finances for the projects He gives them.

There are two pitfalls we should avoid concerning finances:

1. *Recklessness*. A small church has a small budget. Even with a big vision, a small church still has a limited budget. Therefore, its members cannot go out and order everything they would like. Remember it takes time for a vision to manifest.

Sometimes pastors have run ahead and hired or ordered machines, premises and other things which they were not ready to take on. Finding premises which seat 10,000 people when there are only 50 members, is not being full of "faith"—even though you may have a vision for 20,000. Such foolishness will plunge the church into economic difficulties.

There are three areas which must grow together:

1. Members and coworkers.
2. Activities.
3. Premises.

Where these three areas are balanced, and grow in proportion to one another, the church can then tackle the practicalities of its calling. We must consistently walk in faith. This means that we must be certain that God will finance what we are currently doing. We must also have a conviction that God will take care of future projects, even if we do not yet have the finances for them in the natural.

We need to beware of recklessness which is not faith but foolishness. "How marvelous to have huge premises..." Entertaining such thoughts when the time is not ripe is not faith but covetous thinking. Do the premises have to be so large? Is it the ambitious ego that is doing the prompting, or is it the voice of God? If it is from God, is the timing right? If it is God's word and the timing is right, then God will do miracles and there will be no place for fear or uncertainty.

2. Anxiety over finances. This is the second trap. When we overlook the spiritual, we reckon only with visible, tangible resources. Consequently, we are constantly anxious about interest rates, never daring to embark on any project.

Regarding finances, therefore, we must be free of both soulish recklessness and the other extreme, which is anxiety and disbelief.

God Provides for an Attentive Church

Faith for the Church's economic growth should be grounded in what God has said. Everything God has said and planned is also ordered by Him, and whatever He orders, He pays for. Should He order premises, He will pay for them. If He orders smaller projects, He will pay for those too. Therefore, a believer should have a listening ear for what God is saying. Then he will know if God really has said it, when He wants it done, how He wants it done, and whom He has chosen for the task. If the person is thorough and obeys unconditionally, he will not run ahead, nor add or subtract from what God is saying. Then, he can be sure that God will pay the bill! We can have an inner confidence that God will always meet the Church's needs. There will be no need to threaten, pressure, manipulate or cry for the money. Calmly announce the Church's need and then depend upon God to provide it.

A Powerful Deed from the Lord

At the time of writing, our church is celebrating its tenth anniversary. Our first year's budget was US$ 37,500. This year our turnover is around US$ 12 million. In a few years it will reach hundreds of millions. Our organization has steadily grown, in spite of inflation and recession in Sweden.

Attacks on our economy have brought us crises, but God has always acknowledged His work, blessed us and provided us with unceasing help.

During 1985, with a membership of 300, the Lord spoke to us about building new premises. He gave us, among other verses, 2 Kings 6:1,2:

> The company of the prophets said to Elisha, "Look, the place where we meet with you is too small for us. Let us go to the Jordan, where each of us can get a pole; and let us build a place there for us to live." And he said, "Go."

With that and the prophetic word, "Build!" as our foundation stone, God blessed us enormously. Two years later we had a building with 4,000 seats, and a gallery was added the following year, providing a total of 5,500 seats.

Everywhere we went to seek a loan, the answer was the same—"No!" However, God helped us and we collected approximately US$ 2 million. Eventually, after much prayer, one bank allowed us to borrow to complete the building. The whole process was a total miracle, from the collection and the loan, to the building itself. It would take too much space here to describe in detail the wonders which the Lord worked for us during the construction period. But it was a mighty act from the hand of God.

Sweden's largest newspaper wrote: "It is unlikely there will be any building." Yet God made it happen, and many people here were confounded and surprised by it. God kept His word, and everything He ordered was paid for! Later, when the church's expenses soared, He repeatedly worked wonders in protecting, preserving and extending His work. As the work grew, more employees were needed and consequently our expenses increased.

God Pays for Everything He Orders

One department that was very expensive to run was our Christian school. There were very few private schools in Sweden then; those in existence were small and generally faced persecution from the government.

The spirit of socialism which has strongly pervaded Sweden has not encouraged private schools, especially Christian schools. Despite other Scandinavian countries' support of Christian schools, Sweden was unobliging. When we obeyed God's Word, and went ahead with the Christian school, we met immediate resistance from the Socialists. It took two years before the school was officially recognized by the State, which was then administered by the Social Democrats.

At that time, a State subsidy was out of the question. Meanwhile, the school continued to grow, becoming the largest private school in Sweden with ever increasing expenses. This put a strain on the church's economy and finally it became difficult to pay all the bills. What should we do—close the school or abort some other work? When we prayed and went through our various areas of work, we realized that the enemy wanted to destroy the school by trying to starve us out. So we prayed, thanked God, stood on His Word and carried the burden further. Through faith and patience, we received all that was promised. Sweden voted for a new government, a new way of thinking. We were now entitled to receive a government subsidy for our school. (In Sweden, the money for each child's education goes to the school which the child attends.) God performed an economic miracle and the school grew and developed without having to be totally reliant on the church. Again, we saw that since God had ordered the school, He also took care of the payments.

Two years after we built our church premises, God spoke to us about starting Russia Inland Mission. He wanted us to invest US$ 5 million to spread the gospel in Russia over a period of four years. That was almost as much as our whole building cost. The natural question was, where would all this money come from? Shouldn't we use it instead to pay off our mortgage? (We will take up the subject of loans later.) But the Lord encouraged us to seek His kingdom first. He also said, "When you look back you will see that it was, in fact, US$ 5 million." Now four years later, we can look back on the long list of miracles that God has done in Russia. We can see that US$ 5 million were collected and distributed! God keeps His Word. He pays for what He has ordered.

Borrow as Little as Possible

There is nothing in the Bible which says that it is wrong to borrow. However, giving loans is the world's way of keeping people in debt and taking their money. Problems arise when individuals and churches build their whole economy on loans. This becomes dangerous since the borrower is servant to the lender. Therefore, borrow as little as possible and pay off the mortgage as quickly as possible. Loans can be deceptive and cause a church to live beyond her means. The best alternative is to wait, have patience and believe for the money in cash!

There are situations where God sanctions a loan, but then one must make sure that the instalment plan gets underway as soon as possible. Believe God for miracles for the speedy payment of instalments.

Occasionally, a church finds "cash" at the expense of church members and this is not pleasing to God. Some churches have allowed individual church members to take up personal loans or borrow to build for the church's sake. This is a tragic situation which no pastor should allow. Do not put members in debt to boast financial freedom or cover expenses, because that debt has simply been transferred from the church's account to the individual members.

Giving Releases Blessings

God wants to provide for the Church so that it can do everything it is called to do. This requires both faith and commitment. Therefore, teaching on tithing and sacrificial giving should be given to each member. Some preachers have argued that tithing does not belong to the New Testament—it would be interesting to see how much they give to God's work! Every member needs to understand that God is his provider and that He is *able* and *willing* to bless them financially.

The Bible is clear on this point and Jesus says plainly in Luke 6:38 *Give, and it will be given to you.* In other words, God meets our needs when we give toward others' needs, as we see in 2 Cor 9:6 also: *Whoever sows generously will reap generously.*

A church member should not feel that he has been exploited. Instead, he should have understanding, faith and revelation that God *will* bless and help him in every way, including the financial realm. He must understand that it is not just empty words, but a precious revelation.

And God is able to make all *grace abound* to you, so that in *all things at all times, having all that you need,* you will *abound in every good work* (2 Cor 9:8).

This is God's will for every church member. When a believer understands his ministry in this area, financial blessings are released over both his personal life and that of the church.

Sometimes we have heard pastors say out of frustration: "What we need are three or four millionaires to pay our bills." How wrong that is! Three millionaires are not needed. First, we need faith in the pastor's heart. Second, we need correct teaching that builds faith in believers and results in commitment. Furthermore, it was never intended that a few members should carry the whole burden. Everyone should share the weight.

God wants *everyone* to love Him. Everyone should praise Him. All should be intercessors. All should go out with the gospel and all should be givers. This gives strength to a believer's ministry. God does not only want specialists whom we can admire. He seeks an entire group who can rise up, pay the price of commitment and walk with Him. Then great power is released.

God wants everyone to give to His work:

Each man should give what he has decided in his heart to give (2 Cor 9:7).

God expects *every* active believer to be a giver.

Tithing is Instigated by God

When God spoke to His people, He instituted tithing. Even before the Law, Abraham and Jacob gave a tenth of everything (Gen 14:20, 28:22). The principle of tithing is found throughout the Bible. Jesus spoke about it in Matthew 23:23, where he emphasized righteousness and compassion, but tithing was not to be exempt. You should not do one thing and overlook the other. The book of Hebrews also speaks about tithing (Heb 7:2-9). In Malachi 3:6-12, God emphasizes that a tenth *belongs* to Him and that it should be brought into the storehouse. The storehouse is the Church, for it is there one receives food and nourishment.

Ten percent of a person's income belongs to God. That means that he manages better on 90 percent with God's blessings than on 100 percent without God's blessings. When a person does not give his tithe, he robs God of something that belongs to Him. A tenth does not belong to us. It belongs to God.

Giving a tenth to God means that I surrender, sanctify and circumcise my means so that I can safely stand in His covenant where I can count on His blessings. Then, heaven is open over me:

> "Bring the whole tithe into the storehouse, that there may be food in my house. Test me in this," says the Lord Almighty, "and see if I will not throw open the floodgates of heaven and pour out so much blessing that you will not have room enough for it" (Mal 3:10).

Therefore, tithing puts me in a position of protection and blessing.

Joyful Offerings Release
Capital for World Evangelization

God wants me to give offerings, beyond my tithe. I give here according to my faith. As I sow, my return is reckoned to me according to the measure I have used in giving.

This means that God challenges me to be a glad, bold, surrendered giver who gives more than a tenth, but not more than my faith can handle. As a result, God reimburses me with more than I gave Him. The principle of sowing and reaping will operate in my life. This means that the seed sown in my life will give a return of thirty, sixty, or a hundredfold (2 Cor 9:6; Mark 4:20).

In this way, the believer experiences God's laws and principles for economic growth. He experiences God's goodness and blessings and becomes a cheerful giver. He will be a channel of blessing in the area of finances so that the church's work can expand and progress. Then, even a small church can be of great blessing in firmly establishing God's kingdom, while being independent of this world's economic system with its fluctuations and depressions. Above all, Satan cannot use his Mammon system to hinder the Church's work.

God loves every believer. He wants to bless and can afford to bless their wages, as they are His children. But that is not what it is all about. It is not about trying to be rich and live selfishly in the Last Days. Instead, it centers on the Holy Spirit who wants to fill us with faith, release our giving, and free our finances to spread the gospel throughout the earth.

The revival of the Last Days will be the greatest and the most expensive. God is going to finance it, but only as individual believers obey and follow God's plan of giving. A church where half the congregation is lax in tithing closes heaven's blessings over it. However, a church where all give, whatever the level, will experience inexhaustible blessings.

The Bible speaks about cheerful givers. These are believers who are free of economic greed, stinginess, worldliness and poverty mentality. Such a giver constantly sees God's blessings in many different areas. Such a giver has the same heart as God. *For God so loved the world that He **gave**...* (John 3:16). God is a giving, loving and compassionate God.

When the believer has the same heart as God, it is easy for him to give to "all good work." Giving becomes a life-style. Instead of living to get, he lives to give. It becomes more blessed to give than to receive. When that spirit comes over the whole Church, people engage themselves in spreading the gospel everywhere. They give to the poor, they help in times of famine and contribute toward everything that is good. They encourage people while being productive members of society.

A Strong Church
Reestablishes True Lay-workers

We are entering a time when many State social-welfare organizations are starting to collapse. The government and authorities do not have the finances to cushion the impact of economic disaster, no matter how necessary it may be.

Icy financial winds are sweeping across the world. Mammon is a heartless god who does not protect his devotees. But God is able to protect His people and He will do so. Then many social welfare organizations will again be run by strong churches with true, spirit-filled workmen. Compassionate care will be reinstated. Living churches who believe God for supernatural financial blessing will run schools, child care, children's homes. They will have centers for alcoholics and drug addicts, and emergency and disaster programs. They will help the poor, the sick and the elderly. They will provide proper counseling on abortion or unwanted pregnancies, and support broken families, people facing financial ruin, struggling single parents, and much more besides.

Jesus can meet all these needs. His love is endless and there is no limit to what He can do when people make themselves available and have compassionate hearts. Just like the boy who gave his two fish and five loaves, a miracle was released which fed thousands. Jesus wants to meet many people's needs, supernaturally. He will accomplish this through believers who are full of compassion—free, cheerful givers.

7

Persecution and Adversity

The gospel is the power of God for salvation. The Word will bear fruit when it is preached and Jesus promised that we would go out and bear lasting fruit. Therefore, we live in Jesus' victory and believe for breakthrough and success. We believe, according to Psalm 1, that we will prosper in whatever we do. This means victory and success for God's kingdom.

The preacher who neither believes for, nor expects victory, success and growth, will soon be defeated by the enemy. The sword of the Spirit will be wrenched from his hands. He will back into compromise with the world and soon find himself retreating in all areas. This is not God's will. God wants His kingdom to expand everywhere, in and through believers who overcome.

The Gospel's Success Causes Opposition

A study of Acts is a study in the success of the gospel:

> But the word of God continued to increase and spread (Acts 12:24).

> All over the world this gospel is producing fruit and growing (Col 1:6).

The power and the presence of God in the gospel ensured that it bore fruit everywhere. The gospel is still the same. It is just as fruitful and successful right now as it was in the days of Acts. But a price must be paid for that success.

When Paul had preached the gospel in Iconium, Lystra and Derbe, many became believers. The work bore fruit everywhere. But there was also opposition from every quarter. Paul was contradicted, slandered, persecuted and driven away. This did not thwart the gospel's victory but it was Satan's attempt to quench the fire which Paul had lit. So when Paul returned to these churches, it was necessary to encourage and strengthen the disciples.

> They preached the good news in that city and won a large number of disciples. For they returned to Lystra, Iconium and Antioch, strengthening the disciples and encouraging them to remain true to the faith. "We must go through many hardships to enter the kingdom of God," they said (Acts 14:21,22).

Paul explained that they could expect more persecution, just as their salvation had already been resisted. He explained to them that their persecution was not something strange, but part of the Christian life. Their souls, thoughts and emotions had to be strengthened so that they would not lose courage, back down or return to the world.

When a person becomes saved, the gospel is successful and when circumstances are favorable for the gospel, this incurs the wrath of the devil. The believer who has not realized, or refuses to acknowledge that an intense spiritual battle wages about us, has not grasped anything at all.

When you became saved and found peace with God, you automatically became a target for your enemy, the devil. You are no longer in his kingdom or under his influence and he does not like this! When a believer completely surrenders himself to Jesus, follows Him and begins to preach the gospel boldly, the kingdom of Satan starts to lose ground. This provokes him to vent his fury in a counterattack. When we take the initiative, he will meet us head-on and so resistance and persecution are inevitable.

Christianity in the Book of Acts

Many believers say, "If only we had the Christianity of the book of Acts!" They are referring to the abundance of revelation, visions, wonders, signs, powerful miracles, conversions and angelic visitations which characterized that time. This was "supernaturally normal" Christianity and God wants this to be the normal Christian life in the Church today. However, that is not the whole picture of Acts. Together with the signs, wonders and conversions came opposition, persecution, stoning, imprisonment, abuse, flogging, political resistance, injustice and court trials.

Often we want the positive without the negative. We would gladly have large, rich and delicious fruit without being willing to partake in the process that produces the fruit. When we study Acts, we see two sides which are inseparable: success, victory and the presence of God's glory on one hand, and opposition, hate and persecution on the other.

In Acts 4:3 the apostles were arrested and imprisoned.

In 5:18 the apostles were taken into custody.

In 5:27 they were interrogated by the religious authorities.

In 6:12 Stephen was forcefully brought before the Council.

In 7:58 Stephen was driven out of the city and stoned to death.

In 8:1 strong persecution broke out against the church.

In 9:16 Jesus spoke to the newly saved Saul thus: *"I will show him how much he must suffer for my name."*

In 9:24,25 Saul's life was endangered and he fled Damascus hidden in a basket.

In 12:2 James (John's brother) was executed by the sword.

In 13:45-50 Paul was reviled, contradicted and driven away from Antioch.

In 14:5-19 Paul fled Iconium and was stoned in Derbe.

In 16:22-24 Paul was whipped and thrown into jail in Philippi.

In 17:5-10 an uproar broke out in Thessalonica; Paul fled to Berea.

In 18:6 Paul encountered opposition in Corinth. He was reviled by the Jews and brought before the judgment seat (v 12).

In 19:29 an uproar broke out in Ephesus. There was controversy over "the Way" (v 23).

In 21:11 Paul was warned by the prophet, Agabus, of the persecution which would arise in Jerusalem. Rioting broke out in Jerusalem and Paul was imprisoned.

In 22:25 the Romans wanted to take Paul hostage.

In 23:1 Paul stood before the Council as a prisoner and was then taken to prison in Caesarea.

In chapter 24 Paul was brought before the governor, Felix, and was imprisoned for two years.

In chapter 25 Paul was brought before the governor, Festus.

In chapter 26 Paul was brought before King Agrippa.

In chapter 27 Paul was sent as a prisoner to Rome.

In chapter 28 Paul was in Rome. He was opposed, but had liberty to preach.

These difficulties are listed so that you will see these tribulations came with the signs and wonders. Furthermore, you will realize that success is borne through opposition and persecution but that ...*in all these things we are more than conquerors through him who loved us* (Rom 8:37).

It is impossible to understand the gospel and be successful in God's kingdom without meeting opposition from the devil. Therefore, we must be prepared for it.

Confrontation: You Can Count on It!

Some superficial and unbiblical preaching refuses to acknowledge the inevitability of persecution. Their exponents prefer to speak about favor instead. God wants us to have favor with people and it is biblical to believe God for favor. But the Bible mentions favor far less frequently than opposition. That does not mean we should live in anticipation of persecution. No, we believe for and expect victory and success, but opposition is unavoidable. The devil will not sit idly by, watching God's kingdom gain ground. He will do everything to stop the gospel and shoot as many fiery arrows as possible. But praise the name of the Lord for *the shield of faith, with which you can extinguish all the flaming arrows of the evil one* (Eph 6:16).

It is interesting to note that most of Paul's harangues (found in Acts) were not held in churches or synagogues but in courts of law. There was something in the anointing of Paul's ministry that confronted both secular and religious authorities. Spiritual powers which held whole regimes bound in sin, worldliness and religiosity were nervous of Paul's presence. Therefore, there was always resistance and confrontation as people were incited to oppose Paul.

In Acts 17:6, the mob shouts,

"These men who have caused trouble all over the world have now come here."

Acts 17:8 states,

When they heard this, the crowd and the city officials were thrown into turmoil.

Acts 19:23 says,

About that time there arose a great disturbance about the Way.

In Acts 28:22, the Jews' leaders say,

"But we want to hear what your views are, for we know that *people everywhere are talking against this sect.*"

Therefore, if the gospel is preached with power, there will be opposition. But opposition is only temporary. It is there to be overcome. However, it is naive to assume, that we need never encounter opposition. Neither is it prudent to believe that opposition is an indication that we have acted wrongly. On the contrary, it is an indication that we have done something good. When the enemy is shaken and threatened he wants to shut the mouth of the preacher. Therefore he attacks him.

A certain type of superficial faith preaching from America has chosen to reject this aspect of opposition and persecution. Naturally, persecution is never pleasant to the flesh. Everyone wants peace and quiet, comfort and enjoyment, and likes to be appreciated and popular with everyone. These fleshly tendencies will readily adopt a superficial preaching on "having favor" with everyone. The flesh is averse to suffering and surrender and would rather enjoy God's blessings and continue to live its "own life." But this has never been God's intention.

All Christian life is built upon God's Covenant. The Word and the promises of the Covenant coupled with God's commitment to us, are the steadfast foundation in our relationship with Him and our position before Him. In and through Christ, God has really blessed us with all spiritual blessings in the heavenly places (Eph 1:3). Through His Covenant, He has placed everything that He *is*, everything that He *has*, and everything that He *can do* at our disposal. But the Covenant also has another side. God wants us to be committed to Him. He has never intended that His commitment to us and His many blessings should be wasted on a comfortable, fleshly and worldly self-life.

The Lord *has pleasure in the prosperity of His servant* (Ps 35:27, NKJV) and in God's goodness there is no limit to how much He can bless His servant, but it is "His servant" He delights in. A servant is one who submits, obeys, follows and works for his master, Jesus.

> A student is not above his teacher, nor a servant above his master. It is enough for the student to be like his teacher, and the servant like his master. If the head of the house has been called Beelzebub, how much more the members of his household! (Matt 10:24,25).

In His Footsteps: Denial and Blessings

When we follow Jesus, we must deny ourselves. If we are not willing to deny ourselves, we can never seriously follow Jesus. We are only following ourselves and using God as someone who will bless us and help us live in the flesh—but God is not interested in doing that. He has completely committed Himself to us. Therefore, we need to be totally surrendered to Him, so that we can enjoy all the good things which He would give us.

Traditional teaching on denial and surrender has often been in error. A legalistic approach has emphasized that people are never surrendered enough so God begrudges them His blessings. Religious teaching has thus robbed people of something precious, leaving them deeply dejected and gloomy, or legalistic and self-righteous. This is not the will of God.

God wants to pour out His abundance and blessings on His children because He loves us so. However, we cannot preach on God's abundance and blessings in a way that encourages the unrepentant or the carnal Christian to become more egocentric. But when a believer totally surrenders his life to Jesus and means to follow Him on His conditions, then the channels of blessing are opened.

In Mark 10:29,30, Jesus speaks about genuinely following Him:

"I tell you the truth," Jesus replied, *"no one who has left home or brothers or sisters or mother or father or children or fields for me and the gospel will fail to receive a hundred times* as much *in this present age* (homes, brothers, sisters, mothers, children and fields—*and with them, persecutions*) and in the age to come, eternal life."

If a believer is prepared to deny himself for Jesus' sake, he is assured a hundredfold blessing in this age. This hundredfold blessing is God's goodness, abundance and blessings according to His Covenant with His children. But to release these blessings, the believer must deny himself and walk the way of Jesus.

Blessings come during times of persecution. This means that in following Jesus, a believer cannot count on a life of luxury and pleasure, but he will experience tribulation. As promised in His Word, God gives blessing, not frivolous pleasure. This also means that He is not dependent on favorable times to bless His people. He showers His gifts over His children, even in the midst of trials and tribulations. These blessings may even provoke persecution. Carnal Christians and unbelievers can jealously slander and back-bite someone who has received God's blessings.

Persecution and Opposition Produces Glory

God's Covenant has two sides—God's goodness and commitment to us and our commitment to Him. If we see both aspects, then we will have freedom and balance. We will be able to receive everything God wants to give, while understanding that oppression and persecution will attack the believer as the Bible says. All opposition and persecution imply a measure of suffering but it also produces glory.

Believers often make the common mistake of misunderstanding what suffering entails and how it is to be received. We need not carry the suffering which Jesus bore on the cross *for our sakes*. This may include, for example, guilt, sin, sickness, hate and rejection. We may be attacked by these, but in and through the work of reconciliation at Calvary we have the victory! There is forgiveness for the sinner, life in the spirit, healing, deliverance, fellowship and joy in the Holy Spirit. There is a life of victory for us!

However, there is another kind of affliction which we cannot avoid, but which we can nevertheless conquer: that of opposition, apathy, persecution and attacks. We have spiritual weapons to arm ourselves against these attacks, enabling us to further the work of God. We do not have to give up, but as long as we go out with the gospel, the enemy will slander, lie and oppose us. A believer cannot afford to sink into depression in the face of a little opposition. Instead, he should consider it joy, and rejoice in the midst of various trials (Jas 1:2; 1 Pet 1:6).

> *But rejoice* that you participate in the sufferings of Christ, so that you may be overjoyed when his glory is revealed. If you are insulted because of *the name of Christ, you are blessed*, for the Spirit of glory and of God rests on you (1 Pet 4:13,14).

> Blessed are those who are persecuted *because of righteousness*, for theirs is the kingdom of heaven. Blessed are you when people insult you, persecute you and falsely say all kinds of evil against you *because of me*. Rejoice and be glad, because great is your reward in heaven, for in the same way they persecuted the prophets who were before you (Matt 5:10-12).

Jesus spoke of persecution but also of great rewards which are valid for life here on earth, as well as in heaven.

Attacks Originate in the Spirit World

Persecution has never stopped the Church. Worldliness, backsliding and the like have succeeded in halting God's work, but never persecution. Persecution aims to contaminate purity, intimidate God's people and obstruct the preaching of the gospel. We cannot afford to retreat. Instead, we must counterattack and bring down all opposition in the spirit world!

Persecution and opposition do not originate from people, but from the devil. Therefore, we need never fight or be angry with those who suppress the gospel.

> For our struggle is not against flesh and blood, but against the rulers, against the authorities, against the powers of this dark world and against the spiritual forces of evil in the heavenly realms (Eph 6:12).

The unseen powers, the evil principalities of the spirit world which hold people, cities, regions and nations in their grip, are threatened by the preaching of the gospel.

They immediately mobilize their resistance forces to sabotage the power and freedom of the gospel.

> If the world hates you, keep in mind that *it* hated me first. If you belonged to the world, it would love you as its own. As it is, you do not belong to the world, but I have chosen you out of the world. That is why the world hates you (John 15:18,19).

Jesus refers to the world here as "it." He is not pointing the finger at individuals, but He refers to the world as a godless system which keeps people from coming to God. You can have a good relationship with a non-believer and should love and respect all people, whatever their opinions or behavior. But Ephesians 2:2 speaks about the disobedient in this world. They follow the ruler of the kingdom of the air, *the spirit who is now at work in those who are disobedient.* That spiritual power, which is the nature of this world, will always hate, threaten and attack the Church of the living God. It is in this context that Jesus says, *Woe to you when all men speak well of you* (Luke 6:26). God's love should flow through you to all people and they will sense it and like it. However, the gospel will also be a stumbling-block for others and the spirit of this world will inevitably be aggravated.

Persecution from the World

Persecution comes from different directions and takes various forms. It can come from the world, from aggressive individuals as well as from the authorities. Ungodly legislation and hardened, corrupt people holding authority can sometimes do everything in their power to suppress the preaching of the gospel. Often they have no understanding and little interest in the gospel. They heap together all kinds of religious movements and sects and work against all of them. This happens especially in countries with undemocratic governments or countries where socialism predominates.

The Bible says we should pray for the authorities (1 Tim 2:1,2), because even people in positions of authority need to be saved. Furthermore, the Church needs to receive respect and fair treatment. Therefore we should also pray for the mass media which is often State-controlled, since many lies and prejudices are propagated there.

At the same time, believers should not be intimidated by either the press or politicians. The spiritual weapons which God has given the Church are much stronger. A spoken, prophetic word can penetrate into the office of the authorities, resulting in objectivity, humility and change. It is also important for a congregation to expand numerically. A large local congregation has representatives in every area of society. Its thousands of voices certainly have more influence on local and national politicians than a small group of 20 people in a cellar.

However, there has been a reluctance to address authorities. Preachers have often evaded this responsibility by ducking behind a cover of pietism, implying that we should only speak about Jesus and nothing else. We should speak about Jesus for we preach about Him, not politics. We want to promote His truth and love, rather than make spiteful speeches. But God's love is not weak and the gospel that Paul preached often confronted the authorities and caused a stir.

It is not right to live introvertly in an air-tight bubble of piety, while the devil is working overtime to control the nations. The Church must raise her voice before the authorities' godless laws which limit the freedom of the gospel, freedom of speech and freedom to hold meetings. She must pray, preach, prophesy and protest. Right now there is an intense battle waging in Russia, the Ukraine, the Balkans and Eastern Europe. They will either adopt a Western-style democracy or have a system where religious legislation restricts the preaching of the gospel. Unfortunately, many preachers take a low-key stance not wishing to "stir up trouble." In their Western luke-warmness and ignorance of the resulting battle, they inadvertently leave their brothers in the lurch by keeping their pious silence.

Persecution from Backslidden Religious Leaders

Opposition also comes from the backslidden and the religious. When authorities are averse to revival, it is often because they are being ill-advised in religious matters by worldly, spiritually dead, so-called Christians. Often it is these advocates from dead churches and associations who are given much favor in the State-controlled mass media. Their morning devotions, preferences and dissertations are presented to the public as Christianity, while the biblical gospel is presented as the teaching of sects.

Opposition from religious leaders is usually more aggressive than that from the secular world. All backsliders have a peculiar hatred for revival, and for the Lord they have betrayed in exchange for the world's friendship. At the heart of religiosity lies something stronger than many have been led to believe. Its nature is that of a whore who resists, persecutes and hates the living Church. Its champions are often people who have not repented and been born again. However, they have adopted religious opinions, a religious life and acquired influence and status in their particular social sphere. When they meet biblical evangelism, a stark confrontation arises:

- The spirit of this world in religious form is then challenged by the Spirit of God.

- The fleshly self-life, clothed in pious phrases, is challenged by the love of God.

- The worldly, impure, and compromising life is challenged by the holiness and purity of God.

The gospel challenges the soulish, secular, intellectual life.

> The man without the Spirit does not accept the things that
> come from the Spirit of God, for they are foolishness to him,
> and he cannot understand them, because they are spiritually
> discerned (1 Cor 2:14).

Worldly behavior, sin and all reasoning are confronted by
the supernatural life and the gospel, which is the power
of God for salvation.

Concerning Hagar and Sara, Ishmael and Isaac, Paul
says:

> At that time the son born in the ordinary way persecuted the
> son born by the power of the Spirit. It is the same now (Gal
> 4:29).

Confrontation and Opposition
A Part of Revival

Every revival encounters storms and adversity. These
conditions are almost prerequisites for revival and a
consequence of revival. When Elijah exposed Ahab and
confronted ungodliness, the atmosphere was charged for
revival. The lords and elders of the Council persecuted
Peter and the newly-founded Church in a reaction against
the revival of the times.

Some believers mistakenly assume that fresh winds of
revival will blow with renewal, without rocking that which
is old. That is impossible. However, the "old" will not be
challenged just because it is old. The new generation is
not scorning or misunderstanding what an older generation has done. No, it is as Jesus foretold:

> "I sent you to reap what you have not worked for. Others
> have done the hard work, and you have reaped the benefits
> of their labor." (John 4:38).

We should not criticize something simply because it is
old or new. In every revival God has confronted worldliness,
unbelief, sin and dead religiosity. He confronts this in
both its old and new forms. He does this so that the
Church will be pure, holy and spiritually sound. This is
not meant to be directed at older songs, other ordinances

and traditions belonging to certain forms of worship. It is aimed at religious thinking and practices that are not grounded in the Scriptures nor have the Holy Spirit as their instigator.

In this context, if the young can accuse the old of religiosity, then the old can also accuse the young of worldliness. God does not deliver us from bonds of religious bureaucracy so that we become entangled in worldly, fleshly so-called "freedom." He wants us to have spiritual freedom and spiritual life, not worldliness or false religiosity.

Different Levels of Persecution

There are various types of persecution. We often think of the physical kind as being the most severe, but there are three kinds of persecution: physical, mental and spiritual. Mental, soulish persecution comes in unfriendliness, harassment and isolation. If a person is not equipped to meet this, it can cause much suffering. No one wants to be lonely. Everyone wants to be loved and understood. Only Jesus can meet the needs in a person's life. A person can be alone yet still experience God's glory in his life.

On the other hand, if he seeks recognition and fellowship solely from other people, then he loses God's protection and becomes an easy prey for the enemy. Because the need for fellowship and recognition is so strong, some pastors have compromised or remained silent to keep their congregation or remain in their denominations.

If you must choose between truth and fellowship, opt for truth. Choosing truth may cause you to feel lonely at first, but at least you are free, and soon new, true friends will come your way. But if you choose fellowship at the cost of compromising with the truth, you will soon find that your so-called friends have dubious intents. They are only out to defend a religious system and would even force you into conformity and submission. Then you will always feel uneasy inside since you compromised your conscience. If you refuse to compromise and refuse to stoop to this, then God will honor your decision (although you are still fallible) and give you protection against persecution. God gives you a hard forehead but a soft heart (Ez 3:8). That is better than a soft, overly-sensitive forehead and a heart of stone! But hateful words, pride and intellectual disdain, gossip and slander will just bounce back off a hard forehead.

When God's Word comes into a situation, unbelief is exposed. You can either humble yourself as you realize the spiritual implications, repent and be set free, or you can start to fight the light and seek refuge in the shadows. But when you fight the light, you fight God Himself, so you are doomed to failure. If you receive a revelation from the Word concerning something and you preach on it, many more will be blessed by it than will be upset by it. The enemy wants your attention to be focused on all the negative people so that you will be preoccupied with "pie throwing" in the spirit. If you have a truth clarified for you it does not mean that you are faultless. Criticism is always near and ready to pounce on any wrong move you make in order to use this against you. If you have done wrong, confess it before God and do not try to justify yourself before your critics. God knows your heart, and He loves and protects you. He never supports those who constantly find fault or criticize others, talking behind their backs.

Remember that God is your defender, and there are certain "positions" He objects to our holding: those of "accuser" and "judge." Jesus is our defender and we are the "witnesses." God is the judge who tests our hearts. The enemy is the accuser and fortunately, we are not called to stand in for him!

The highest form of persecution is spiritual persecution. This occurs when a hostile spiritual prince takes a personal stand against you, your church and your work. The oppression is felt in the whole atmosphere. It comes against the preacher as complete hopelessness. It feels like cold steel in the air, numbness, heaviness, drowsiness, hate, wrath or strong control and isolation.

Elijah experienced this when Jezebel turned her rage upon him. After his heroic actions and being used by God to do a mighty miracle, he suddenly wanted to give up, flee and die. This type of attack has always come against leaders of revival to intimidate, isolate and finally destroy them. Paul also suffered affliction because of the extremely high revelations he received and an angel of Satan struck him (2 Cor 12:7).

But *in* and *through* these attacks there is victory. If you have victory over fear and loneliness, over compromise and worldliness, then persecution cannot injure you. Instead, it only confirms that what God does is right and the enemy is threatened and nervous.

God Can Turn Persecution into Good

When we started our church in 1983, we immediately encountered opposition and persecution. This developed into one of the biggest opposition movements seen in Scandinavia for many years. Satan's stronghold of world-liness and religiosity was being threatened in a way it had not known for a long time. Such intense, frequent attacks and lies from both the secular and religious mass media had not been seen since the Pentecostal Revival reached Scandinavia at the beginning of the century. Yet God was compassionate and merciful and we felt His comfort, strength and glory over the church.

About ten theologians were present at the meeting where the church was officially declared. The opposition in the spirit world was so intense that I could not recall what I had said during the first ten minutes I preached. I had to go home and listen to the tape to remember it. Yet when the church was being proclaimed through the many confessions, the pressure in the spirit world was broken.

When our Bible school started it was the biggest Bible school in Sweden from the first year. Therefore it received a great deal of media attention. For guest speakers from other countries, particularly the USA, this was an unusual phenomenon. They were not used to that type of publicity and the subsequent opposition. Their spiritual environment was so different that some found it difficult to grasp what happens when God wants to arouse a whole nation to speak to it. From the beginning, we sensed strongly that God wanted to awaken and shake the nation. Many believers agreed with this, but perhaps not with the price that had to be paid for it.

Television followed our development suspiciously. Religion had almost departed from the public arena, and had faded from the educational system into retirement—an antique belonging to an old homestead museum. One TV program featured our church. That program oozed hatred, prejudice, and lies. But when the church members viewed it, they did not lose courage, although they knew it would evoke hatred in the minds of the Swedish people. The Holy Spirit said, "All the garbage they throw at you will pile up high. I am going to turn that pile into a platform from which you can preach to the whole country."

A few years later, the Lord gave us a TV church service on a popular Swedish State channel. Afterwards, a well-known journalist interviewed me for a whole hour on a high-rating TV program. What had happened? God had taken the persecution and used it for something positive. We had gained the public's attention in a unique opportunity to present Jesus to the Swedish people!

Prophetic Confrontation
Changes the Spiritual Atmosphere

For many years, the Socialists in Sweden have resisted the gospel. Gradually, they de-Christianized the schools and secularized the country. Through the State Church and theological faculties, Christianity became antiquated and the Church conformed to worldly ideals.

Sweden has become one of the most atheistic countries in the world. Yet God still wants to do the miraculous, heal the sick, cast out demons and save our people. The enemy has furtively taken over many areas of life in Sweden, more so than in many other countries. No wonder we experienced the enemy's retaliation—as well as the wonderful victories!

During a Summer conference in 1985, the Holy Spirit directed me to speak to the spiritual power of lawlessness behind atheistic socialism. I preached on Sweden and the Swedish flag, declaring: "The yellow cross is the glory of Jesus' reconciliatory work and the resurrection. The blue background is heaven and God's prophetic word." In this context I said two things which caused quite a stir: "Socialism is of the devil" and "We need a new government." The 4,000 conference participants prayed in a wonderful and powerful unison for deliverance and revival in Sweden. Immediately afterwards, an outcry broke out in various camps throughout the land. Furthermore, it was election year!

We are not called to preach politics, but there are certain truths which we are sometimes afraid to touch. If we prophetically give voice to what God wants, it will set off a chain reaction, and its result will be seen in the years ahead.

Sweden is different today, in both the spiritual and secular areas, and true revival is imminent. That revival is worth whatever it costs. Favor and breakthrough follow victory over opposition. God can totally change a country's spiritual climate. All forms of privation and resistance cause change, and that means a national breakthrough. Therefore, it is wonderful to see an increasing change in the spiritual climate of Sweden, as people are becoming more open to the gospel.

Persecuted for Your own Stupidity

Persecution comes because one is a Christian, loves Jesus and stands for God's Word. This does not cover persecution which comes after making a fool of oneself by fleshly behavior, or provoking negative reactions by being stubborn, immature and carnal. Wise behavior wins favor without having to stoop to compromise or cowardice, because it stems from a genuine love and sensitivity for the unsaved.

Sometimes believers think they can display their spirituality by roaring in tongues in department stores! They enforce their witness on colleagues during working hours or hold prayer meetings in apartments which wake up the whole building at 2 am! This would sooner lead to persecution for illegal conduct rather than for the gospel's sake. God's love for people comes as a burden for souls. This results in true wisdom which wins respect.

> When a man's ways are pleasing to the Lord, he makes even his enemies live at peace with him (Prov 16:7).

Joseph, Daniel and Nehemiah are examples of godly men who experienced both persecution and opposition, and grace and favor with various peoples. Through it all, God was with them. They the won victory, and the work which God had set for them was accomplished. The enemy could not stop them. The same applies to Paul. In his last letter he wrote of his resistance and persecution as well as having kept the faith, finishing the race and winning the victory (2 Tim 4:7). No adversity could hinder him. He achieved all that God had wanted him to do.

8

The Believer's Ministry in the Church

The Church can be portrayed as God's temple, God's peculiar people, the body of Christ, God's family and God's army. Each aspect relates to the individual's function and place within this body.

When a person is saved, he is placed in the body of Christ. He is placed where God wants him to be, which is not his own choice, but God's choice. This also applies to the local church where he should belong. He cannot have a casual relationship with his church. The Church is God's family and God wants each believer to have the same sense of identity in the Church as he has in his own home. He knows he belongs there. He is secure because it is his base. It is a place where he can work, rest, rejoice and cry.

The Lord places a believer in the local church so that he will grow and find his work and identity there. He needs to come into the most powerful service on earth—the service of the believer.

Don't Despise the Believer's Ministry

Believers often want ministerial gifts because they need to feel successful and accepted. This is totally wrong! God wants believers to be strong in the supernatural without necessarily being employed full-time. The believer already has a full-time ministry, often without realizing it. He has a social network of neighbors, friends, work colleagues and relatives which is often wider than that of the preacher. Therefore, it is tragic when a believer becomes passive and lives solely through meetings, hoping that the preacher will do all the work.

No matter how anointed a preacher may be in a meeting, he cannot lead any more unsaved people to Christ than those whom the believers have brought with them!

God wants every believer to discover, appreciate and develop the ministry and the anointing that he already has. He should not just sit quietly in the pew, admiring the preacher and wishing that he were like someone else.

Jesus said, referring to believers, *"These signs will accompany those who believe"* (Mark 16:17). He then listed baptism in the Spirit (speaking in tongues), deliverance and healing. All this should be part of every believer's life. The various ministerial gifts are there to serve and develop the Church, so that every believer finds his full potential in God. However, we need a vision of the Church's identity and the believer's place in the body of Christ to enable this to happen:

- If the Church is a *spiritual temple,* the believer is a living stone.

- In the *body of Christ,* the believer is a limb.

- Among a *kingly priesthood,* the believer is a king and a priest.

- Among a *people of God,* the believer is a citizen.

- In the *army of God,* the believer is a soldier.

- In the *family of God,* the believer is a child.

- In *God's garden,* the believer is a precious plant.

- As part of a *grape-vine,* the believer is a branch that bears fruit.

The believer's ministry is not some secondary service but a vital, primary ministry. Sometimes so much attention is given to the five ministerial gifts that the ministry of the believer is overlooked.

Anointing Follows Obedience

All ministry goes back to Jesus. He is our role model in everything. The Lord's Spirit was on Him (Luke 4:18) to empower Him to preach, heal and deliver. Today, through the Holy Spirit, that same anointing has come upon the whole body of Christ. Each individual is anointed to serve and do the works of Jesus. This comes through the new birth and baptism in the Holy Spirit.

Nowhere is it written that only the preacher or the priesthood are spiritual ministers. Jesus says,

> "I tell you the truth, anyone who has faith in me will do what I have been doing. He will do even greater things than these, because I am going to the Father" (John 14:12).

Every believer is called to live a supernatural life with Jesus. He should see signs and wonders working in his own life and personally carry God's power to others. That is why it is vital to find your place in the body of Christ.

We must understand that God's power, anointing and blessing come through obedience. Jesus is not only our personal Savior, but Lord over His body, the Church. And the universal Church's manifestation throughout history is the local church. Therefore, the individual believer must come into the obedience of faith. He should confess Jesus as his Lord in the local church, where he will find protection, security, blessings and assignments.

If a believer preaches from his "own ministry" alone, separates himself or refuses to join a local church, it will lead to weakening, confusion and rebellion. God has a place for everyone in a strong, growing, and living church. There, each believer finds his appointed tasks. Love, faithfulness and unselfishness are tested. Character is built up and gifts are developed. There, he enters the fullness of his calling.

Many think that they will lose their individuality when they give themselves over to work in a local church. But such wrong thinking is built upon fear and selfishness. When a believer dares to find his place, the anointing which flows through the whole church will strengthen, sharpen, protect and develop each person's life in God.

> From him the whole body, joined and held together by every supporting ligament, grows and builds itself up in love, as each part does its work (Eph 4:16).

The believer must deal with his own rebellion, worldliness and self-will, and then put down roots where Jesus has planted him. Then he will begin to grow. He will no longer be merely a consumer of meetings and conferences. He will be a vital link, helping and strengthening the church, not just selfishly taking all the time. Then the power and anointing which belongs to his particular work will flow.

Each believer has a special task and God has a measure of anointing for that particular work. When the believer enters this and grows in it, he finds fulfilment, security and job satisfaction. Then the church becomes a place where everyone works, grows and does the work of Jesus.

The Ministerial Gifts Develop the Believer

> It was he who gave some to be apostles, some to be prophets, some to be evangelists, and some to be pastors and teachers (Eph 4:11).

The ministerial gifts are for building up believers, strengthening their spiritual life and helping them to fulfill their own ministry. These ministers are not prima donnas who are to be held in awe and admired like self-centered actors! They are like mechanics who fix a car so that it can be driven forwards without any problem.

The ministerial gifts are gifts to the church and should be respected and appreciated. (Some pastors have been pushed down and treated very badly by the elders and the church). But they are not celebrities to be idolized. They are workers, placed there by God to strengthen the believers and *to prepare God's people for works of service, so that the body of Christ may be built up* (Eph 4:12).

All the Ministerial Gifts
were Working in Jesus' Ministry

- Jesus is the *apostle* and high priest of our confession (Heb 3:1).

- Jesus is the *prophet* who should come (Deut 18:15).

- Jesus is the *evangelist* who preached, healed and delivered (Matt 9:35).

- Jesus is the *good shepherd* (John 10:11).

- Jesus is the *teacher* who taught the people (Matt 5:1,2).

The Spirit of the Lord was over Jesus to enable Him to do all these things. Then Jesus gave these gifts to the Church to build it up, and part of this anointing is on each believer. Every believer is sent out (that is the meaning of the word "apostle"). Every believer can prophesy, evangelize and witness. Every believer should care for other believers and help them—that is what a shepherd does. Every believer should know the Scriptures and let the Word of God dwell richly in his heart. He should encourage, admonish and share the Word with others.

Besides all this, the believer is empowered through the baptism of the Holy Spirit so signs and wonders can operate through his life.

Kings and Priests

Every believer is king and priest. 1 Peter 2:9 says that we are a *royal priesthood* and we should all *declare* (His) *praises*.

Each believer is very precious in the sight of God. He is part of a holy, peculiar people who belong to God. He is not a problem sitting in a corner, but someone chosen to live as a citizen in a nation under God.

The believer should enjoy his God-given spiritual identity. When he became aware of his sin against God and repented with all his heart, he was saved. He was cleansed in the blood of Jesus, given a right position before God and justified in Christ Jesus. He gained peace with God and was no longer an enemy to Him. God's Spirit came over him and he was born again. He became a new creation in Christ Jesus. A new inner man was born, making him a child of God.

Now he no longer belongs to the world, or Satan's kingdom and he is no longer mastered by sin. He is now a citizen in God's kingdom, where Jesus is Lord and King.

In that kingdom he is exalted to king and priest. This is not in himself, according to the old nature, nor after the flesh, but on the foundation of Jesus' blood, Jesus' justification and the grace of God. As a new creation in Christ, he has a new identity and a new position. He now sits with Christ in heaven.

But he also has a walk of faith here, on earth. He walks in the spirit and lives a sanctified life which goes from glory to glory. Here on earth the devil, the flesh, the world and sin constantly try to obstruct spiritual growth. They try to hinder the inner life from manifesting outwardly, bearing fruit and working for the expansion of God's kingdom.

But the new life is not meant to be lived alone. The right place for it is in a living church. There the believer is king and priest, a member of God's special people.

Reigning in the Spirit World

We are in a God-given position to rule like kings. The dominion which man lost at The Fall is regained in the new birth. This is man's position in Christ. He is an obedient king under Christ, who is King of Kings. He is not a half-god or a "mini pope."

The kingly reign God gives him is not power over other people. He should love and serve other people, but he also has a position of authority in the spirit world.

The kingly position in Christ means that just as a king commands and gives orders, so the believer has authority in the name of Jesus, to resist Satan. He can speak out

God's words, thoughts and plans. He can give prophetic directives. He can pray and make requests in Jesus' name, take control over circumstances, and request that God's kingdom expand and that God's will be done.

The Church has sovereign authority through its power to loose and bind. Jesus says,

"Whatever you bind on earth will be bound in heaven, whatever you loose on earth will be loosed in heaven" (Matt 16:19).

Believers have failed to acknowledge the kingly side of their ministry. But this sphere is enormous. Jesus says,

"I have given you authority to trample on snakes and scorpions and *to overcome all the power of the enemy;* nothing will harm you" (Luke 10:19).

Set Apart to Minister before God

Just as there is a kingly aspect to the believer's ministry, there is also a priestly aspect. This advocates our coming into the presence of God and ministering there before Him. It is very important to highlight this aspect:

1. Priests should be set apart for God.

Therefore, I urge you, brothers, in view of God's mercy, to offer your bodies as living *sacrifices,* holy and pleasing to God—which is your spiritual *worship* (Rom 12:1).

If a believer does not live a holy, sanctified life his kingly authority will not operate. Instead of receiving answers to prayer, his flesh will take over and produce dead works. Therefore, the believer must live in priestly separation. His life is a living sacrifice to God as he is set apart for a holy ministry.

When priests in the Old Testament were separated for God, they took off their personal clothes and put on the priests' vestments. The focus was not on any individual, but on God, who was central. Thousands of priests worshiped God daily in the temple. We don't even know their names because that was not important. God alone was in the center, not the priests.

2. After the priests were sanctified and separated, they would make the daily sacrifices. The offerings of the various sacrifices were scrupulously prescribed by the Law. It pictured the exactness of God and His expectation of His people to obey Him in every detail and instruction.

The daily sacrifices represent the believer's daily struggle against the flesh. We are dead to the world and Romans 8:12 says that we have no obligation to the flesh. Each day the priests took animals—which are living flesh—killed them, burnt them and offered them to God. Each day, the believer metaphorically takes "living flesh," kills and sacrifices it to God. He lives not in the flesh but in the spirit: *but if by the Spirit you put to death the misdeeds of the body, you will live* (Rom 8:13).

3. The priests praised and worshiped God daily with song and music. That is a picture of the believer's ministry according to Hebrews 13:15: *Through Jesus, therefore, let us continually offer to God a sacrifice of praise—the fruit of lips that confess his name.*

4. The priests were continually before God making intercession for the people. That is a picture of each believer's ministry of intercessory prayer for the Church and for the lost. Those who only pray for their own needs have no understanding of their position as a holy priesthood.

5. The priests preserved the sacred by taking care of the holy objects. This represents the spiritual vigilance all believers must have, so that the flesh and the world do not take over and the holy presence of God disappears.

6. The priests lectured on the Law to the people. Similarly, all believers should communicate God's Word and truth to others, so that the people are not destroyed from *lack of knowledge* (Hos 4:6).

God's Glory is Manifested through His Holy People

The purpose of each different part of the priestly ministry was to establish the holiness of God among His people.

God is a holy God, and only when His people are holy can His presence and glory be manifested among them. God never goes the way of the flesh and the world, since the world and the flesh are opposed to Him:

> The sinful mind is hostile to God. It does not submit to God's law, nor can it do so (Rom 8:7).

The ways of the flesh always oppose the ways of God. God can never tolerate our rebellion against Him. Therefore, the flesh must be sacrificed and the believer yielded to the obedience of faith. He must abdicate from the throne of his self-centered, soulish life and take Jesus as his Lord and Messiah, as his King who is anointed to lead and decide.

> Make every effort to live in peace with all men and to be holy; without holiness no-one will see the Lord (Heb 12:14).

God wants us to see Him, to see Jesus, His glory, His wonder and His manifested presence. But it will never happen through the ways of the world and the flesh, but only through faith, holiness and consecration. God dwells among His people, but His is always a holy presence.

God wants to show Himself to the world, but it is in the temple, the Church, that His glory is manifested. Therefore, He needs a sanctified people who both minister before Him in priestly service, and convey His Word and His powerful works through kingly authority. Through all this they love the world and give freely of themselves so that people will come to salvation.

People come to the church with different backgrounds. They will be at different stages in their spiritual growth and maturity. For this reason, the Church is not a place for a "spiritual elite," but a place for everyone. God loves everyone and He wants each person to develop and grow, spiritually. On the other hand, the Church should not resemble a worldly institution where the flesh governs every development.

Therefore, the shepherd's work is grounded in these three functions:

1. To lead.
2. To feed.
3. To protect.

Sometimes, he may have to act and make decisions which are generally not well received. He should love and help everyone, but he cannot feed people's flesh to promote his own popularity.

After a while he will learn that people differ in their attitudes and motives. Therefore, a shepherd must be free from the need to gain popularity; otherwise he could never correctly admonish and help people grow. Moreover, he would only come near them in their flesh.

Attacks which Threaten
a Church's Unity and Strength

God wants His Church to be united. It need not be perfect, but it should be united. The devil will try his best to split the Church so that it will be weak and ineffective. Therefore, each church will be subject to various attacks from sources within and without. We can list them as follows:

1. *Resistance to evangelism.* There are always those who do not want or dare to tell of Jesus. If such people dominate the church, it will either become introverted or worldly. Nothing enlivens believers so much as telling others of Jesus.

2. *Resistance to prayer.* Usually, there are fewer participants at prayer meetings than at Sunday services. Why? Because prayer costs. When the enemy attacks, prayer is often the first to disappear. It is impossible to build a spiritually strong work if a spirit of prayer does not rest over the whole church and not just over two intercessors.

3. *Resistance to outward manifestations of spiritual freedom.* Some believers are more interested in keeping their dignified bearing than letting the Holy Spirit's will come through. Others are so ignorant or afraid of the Spirit's manifestation that they immediately brand every-

thing as "extreme." Therefore, the shepherd must be secure and dare to let the Holy Spirit work in different ways. He should instruct his people on the various manifestations so that they do not fear or despise such things which the fleshly mind cannot control or understand.

4. *Wrong teaching*. There are many examples of this, and we have already named a few in a previous chapter. Teaching should be broad, fundamental and faith-building. Jesus, the cross and grace must be central. "Christ is the heart and star of the Scriptures," said Luther. From the central point a light can shine on the lesser parts, but not vice versa. Sometimes the preaching needs to be strong and challenging. But if listeners are constantly told how bad and inadequate they are, and how far from revival they are, it will only nurture unbelief, despondency and contempt. God is positive and inspires people so that they can grow further.

5. *Lack of exhortation*. If a garden is never weeded, it will soon be choked with weeds. Worldliness, gossip, slander, apathy, uncleanliness and rebellion must be dealt with; otherwise these things will soon choke the church. If one does not arrest sin in any given situation, success and blessings will soon stop.

6. *Rebellion*. There are many examples in the Bible showing how sin blossomed into outright revolt. Moses encountered this often and he knew the taste of the people's revolt. He met rebellion from Aaron and Miriam when they were jealous that God spoke more often to him than to them. He experienced the rebellion of Korah and Dathan when they accused him of making himself superior to the assembled people. Ten of the twelve scouts started a rebellion and won the support of the people. He experienced everything and survived it all.

It is written of Moses that he was the most humble man on the face of the earth. Although he had periods of despondency, he was so certain and secure in his calling that he never lost balance. He never fled. He never railed accusations at the people. He never defended himself.

God was with him always. When God wanted to strike the people, Moses intervened and entreated God on their behalf. That was the way to victory and the way out of rebellion. The real instigator of rebellion is Satan. He wants to be like God and equal with Him. That is why he fell (Isa 14:12-15).

Rebellion Against Church Leadership

God is particular about His ordinances. He loves everyone equally, but rebellion is never acceptable to Him. Rebellion comes when Satan puts jealousy, pride or a critical spirit into the heart of someone against the pastor or the leadership. The devil is always out to take high positions.

There is a spiritual power—the spirit of Jezebel—which is a fawning, manipulative spirit. It aims for the leadership and wants to take over through threat or manipulation to control God's people and destroy the prophetic anointing. Such was the character of Queen Jezebel and the spirit which motivated her actions. It will rebel against those whom God has placed in leadership and try to replace them with people who do not have that calling. This spirit despises and maligns the person whom God has anointed. It wants to see him replaced by someone else who would work against the anointing and impose power, control and worldliness instead.

When a pastor detects rebellion, he should not react in the flesh. He does not have to defend himself against any criticism or contempt which is shot at him. Rebellion often comes from people who have had long-term designs to reach the top and take over. They readily say, "I've been here since the beginning," or, "I am called of God to stand next to the pastor," or, "I must help the pastor. He has so many incapable workers." They often fire criticism at people on the same level as themselves or those below them, while also feigning affection and currying favor in order to climb to a higher status. Such people are never at peace. They lack a servant-heart and are always proud, scornful and critical. They are also eager to gather about themselves a group of followers who are weak-natured and fleshly-minded. These people constantly feed them with assurance that they are indeed the most anointed.

If a shepherd overlooks this and allows such people to go unchecked, the whole church will soon be infiltrated. When he takes a stand against them, he will be strongly criticized for being "hard," "insensitive," "lacking in love" and "wanting in anointing." Those who criticize and cause rebellion usually take a few supporters and leave the church with much ado and commotion. Their leaving, however, is preferable to their taking control.

These spirits of rebellion usually leave in bitterness, self-pity, criticism and gossip. They must restlessly telephone others and infect them, reaffirming their negative attitudes. But meet them some time after they have left the church and it will be evident that they are not winning the lost, not attending prayer meetings and not studying the Scriptures. They are preoccupied with slander and their fleshly self-life. They are wasting their energies, losing power and eventually disappearing altogether from a life with God. Tragic!

Rebellion and constructive criticism are two different things. The pastor who cannot tolerate any questioning and takes every objection personally is inviting trouble. This also applies when the congregation has no insight into the administration of church affairs, especially those concerning finances.

The Church and Democracy

The Church has sometimes been accused by secular society or religious institutions of being undemocratic. Therefore, it is vital to understand what "democracy" means.

In a free society, decisions are made in a spirit of democracy. There is understanding and tolerance toward minority groups, within an established framework, in which freedom of opinion, freedom of religion and other fundamental freedoms are protected. The Church, which is "the pillar and foundation of truth" will always be the salt and light which secures and maintains these rights. Wherever biblical revival and preaching of the gospel have been oppressed, society is invariably marked by various forms of dictatorship. We find this phenomenon occurring in the former East European countries, where the Orthodox and Catholic State churches are now trying to gain control of the governments. They want to stop all forms of evangelization and impose laws of religious monopoly and intolerance to obstruct every form of revivalist Christianity.

When the Church upholds the fundamental rights of democracy, it does so from a totally different basis to that of secularized society. Society has no objective basis of truth on which to stand. "Everything is relative" and majority consensus is the only yardstick for measuring what is true. Popular opinion, however, is not necessarily truth. A law is not necessarily right just because 51 percent believe it to be so and vote for it, overriding the opinion of the remaining 49 percent. When a parliament votes for a measure and it becomes law, the Church may recognize that law without necessarily finding it acceptable.

The Church must accept society's democratic rules, which are basic to the legislation of the land. But one need never approve ungodly legislation. This does not mean that believers become anarchists. However, they should have the liberty and God-given opportunity to cry, *O land, land, land, **hear** the word of the Lord!* (Jer 22:29). The Church has what the de-Christianized, secularized world lacks: a fundamental basis of truth. The Church knows—when it has the Bible as its foundation and is open to revelation—that some things are true and some are not. These matters cannot be voted on.

When secularized society or worldly Christians say that people should vote on everything, the Church answers thus: "We cannot vote on God's Word. We do not vote on God's existence. We do not vote on whether the Bible is God's Word or not. We do not vote on Jesus' resurrection, the virgin birth or miracles. We receive what God says and accept it as the foundation for our lives. The gospel, Jesus' reconciling death and resurrection, the Word and the work of the Holy Spirit are the fundamental truths for our faith and our lives. Therefore, we do not unquestioningly swallow everything in blind faith. We should test all things."

> Now the Bereans were of more noble character than the Thessalonians, for they received the message with great eagerness and examined the Scriptures every day to see if what Paul said was true (Act 17:11).

> Brothers, stop thinking like children. In regard to evil be infants, but in your thinking be adults (1 Cor 14:20).

Do not treat prophecies with contempt. Test everything. Hold on to the good (1 Thess 5:20,21).

Affirm Everything Jesus Says to the Church

Every believer has the right to prove everything which is taught. The shepherd who intimidates and threatens church members who do not immediately agree with him in everything, has not understood his position. He cannot rush out with "Touch not God's anointed!" Nor can he question certain believers' spiritual lives just because they do not lend their total support. This is dangerous spiritual encroachment.

There are various pitfalls here. The shepherd must realize that not everyone will always understand that something is from God. At times he must wait patiently and walk with the sheep. A prophetic message can be provocative and premature, but if it is from heaven, it will be fulfilled and the people will recognize it and understand. On the other hand, members need to weigh their own hearts to see if their negativity is from the flesh. They need to see whether they are standing in the obedience of faith and following Jesus. If so, they can discern between the various phenomena out of their own spirits, and not out of fleshly criticism, rebellion or worldly rationale.

This means that *both* the leadership and members have a responsibility to submit themselves to the Chief Shepherd, Jesus. They should test everything and affirm everything Jesus says and wants to see in the Church, from that position of submission and obedience. This is, of course, incomprehensible to the unsaved. They do not believe in God's existence. They do not respect biblical ground, nor believe that God can speak to a church or into a believer's life. To the spiritual person, however, it is obvious.

So there is balance between faith and obedience, freedom and responsibility. When church members see God's spoken word come to pass just as God said it would, faith for the leadership grows and co-operation increases. When the shepherd sees the members testing his words, taking them to heart and submitting themselves to what Jesus said, he holds them in higher esteem.

God places the same word in the shepherd's heart and the members' hearts. He wants all to be of one mind. The shepherd is not a dictator who barks commands, threatens and manipulates so that people will follow and obey him. Instead, the Church becomes a people who together hear and obey the Lord's word. Then they rejoice together over reports of growth, wonders and break-through, and praise God for everything He does.

So keep the congregation informed, preferably in specific meetings for church members. Then, all members can participate, understand and have confidence in everything that happens. After all, it is their time, their involvement, their sacrifices and their money which enable it to take place. When a project is presented, it gives every believer the opportunity to discern it to see if it really is God's will.

This is the highest form of democracy. God always wants people to link themselves to Him and His work—never by force, threat or manipulation—but through their *free will*. When a church plans to build, each member votes his support through his involvement, prayer and co-operation with the project. This creates a powerful unity that allows space for personal integrity and responsibility. Furthermore, it releases immense power and achieves supernatural results!

When all this evolves in love and unity, a wonderful fellowship is nurtured in the church. All feel that they play a part in the same family and each takes his responsibility. When inevitable mistakes are made— whether by the shepherd or the members—love flows regardless and the work will continue to grow out of a strong base.

In any vast project, mistakes and wrong decisions will be made, but where everyone's heart seeks God, God's blessings will reside over the work and it will grow. But where criticism, jealousy, disorder or pride begin to flourish, decision-making will be fleshly, wrong ambitions will emerge and the work will begin to crumble.

"Let Us Rise Up and Build"

The shepherd must realize that all people, including himself—no matter how spiritual they are—make mistakes. That is not meant to evoke fear, despondency or contempt, but rather, to prepare the shepherd to flow continuously in forgiveness and persevering love (toward himself as well). He should believe God's promises that He has His hand over the church and He will let it grow.

Similarly, the individual believer should not get caught up in negative attitudes and become critical when he discovers that people are not perfect in his church. Even he is not perfect! The congregation is like a construction. Therefore, a person who criticizes them for not having a roof when they are only at the stage of laying the foundation would be ungracious indeed! He should come and join in the work. Then, not only would the roof be raised, but soon the wallpaper would be pasted and the windows adorned with flowers as well.

That was what we noticed in our church. Certain things were missed at the beginning, and people complained, but eventually everything fell into place. God has His timetable. He knows when, where and how everything should come into place. Those who contribute toward the work will see it appear and see all needs gradually met. But armchair critics and complainers will never partake of the joy and blessings.

Each member should say in his heart, the words of Nehemiah's coworkers: *"**Let us** rise up and build"* (Neh 2:18, NKJV).

Then it will be as Nehemiah said, *"The God of heaven, himself will prosper us; therefore we His servants will arise and build, but you have no heritage, or right or memorial in Jerusalem"* (Neh 2:20, NKJV).

9

God's Plan for the Church —a Base for Revival

The Church's ultimate goal is revival and its fruit is the manifestation of God's presence and glory among His people. Revival involves restoration and reformation. It shakes society, and brings salvation to the people. Furthermore, God wants all this to be achieved through His Church. No wonder the devil loathes the Church and continually attacks it!

When we think of revival, we often think of mass revival where thousands of people find salvation. That is revival in its broadest sense. But strictly speaking, the definition of revival is to rouse the Church out of backsliding, worldliness and sin to an active, living faith and true obedience. This results in God's presence, glory and wonder being seen among His people. It brings salvation and growth, and establishes God's Word and the Holy Spirit's influence in all areas of life.

This enormous task is impossible for man, but God can perform it and He will do so. Revival will shake the world, and the Church will carry it through, before Jesus returns!

Revival can generally be summarized in three words:

1. *Revival*—salvation of people.

2. Reformation—its effect on society, involving the restoration of all that has been broken down.

3. Restoration—the restoration and renewal of the Church in all its forms and functions as described in the Bible, namely:

a) Doctrine—the foundations are reestablished.

b) Life-style—the believer returns to a holy life style.

c) Power—the norm is the supernatural.

d) Order—ministries, gifts, anointing and offices operate in harmony in the body of Christ.

We are now in an accelerating process of restoration, which will continue until Jesus returns. When Jesus comes, He will not find a defeated, confused and depressed little flock. He will find a Church filled with power, glory, faith and obedience, bearing much fruit throughout the world. Revelation will be restored to the Church. Then, every spiritual victory, every biblical duty and every form of true, spiritual life will combine to form a mighty temple of God, ready for Jesus' return. The Church will be all God has intended her to be.

All this can only take place through revival, reformation and restoration and then the farmer will be able to gather the precious produce of the soil (Jas 5:7). There will be an explosion in the body of Christ which will increasingly gain strength as the pure, virgin Church separates herself from religious harlotry and worldly influence. The Church will then emerge resplendent and ready to complete her End-time mission, immediately before Jesus' return. Then the Church Age closes, and a new age—The Millennium—begins!

Revival Puts God in the Center

There has been a great deal of discussion about revival and its causes and consequences. There is both a divine and a human side in revival. We should always evangelize, but revival is more than evangelization. God works in people's hearts so that they are drawn to Jesus. God has made Himself dependent upon people to prepare, organize and complete revival. He accomplishes all this *through* His servants, but the work itself is *His*.

Throughout revival, God is always at the center, while people, however anointed and mightily used, are the back-up staff. Revival is a manifestation of God's presence, personality and character, and of His holiness and power, a power most unexpected and irresistible.

When revival comes, it penetrates society, changing individuals and changing the Church. A new wind of life and freedom blows over mankind. Satan's influence is broken, the powers of darkness flee, and humanity is lifted to an unprecedented height. Blessings flow through every area of life, and the true meaning of life is understood. Mankind is to serve and glorify God here on earth, and then, live with Him in the eternal life to come.

In the fullness of revival, the eternal becomes tangible, and temporal things seem less significant. Heaven is visiting earth! God is confronting society. Revival is God's gift to *every* generation, and no believer in any nation should give in before revival manifests in their time.

Revival will always differ throughout history. There is no need to imitate a previous revival's shape and style, but nonetheless, the inner content, spirit and direction will be the same. The whole Bible gives testimony of revival, as does Church history. One of the mightiest revivalist preachers ever, Charles Finney, defined revival as, "Neither more nor less than a new beginning of obedience to God's Word."

Revival Penetrates Sin and Points to Grace

Revival has certain characteristics:[*]

1. Revival comes at times of deep moral decay.

2. It has always begun in the contrite heart of a servant of the Lord.

3. Its foundation is always the Word of God.

4. It has always resulted in people returning to true worship of God.

5. It has always resulted in the pulling down of idols and false security.

6. In every revival people removed themselves from sin.

---

[*] Fischer—Reviving Revivals.

7. In every revival joy and freedom were renewed and restored.

8. The result of every revival has been national prosperity.

The onset of revival is always met by commotion and confrontation. At that point, preaching should be straight-forward, effective and must penetrate people's hearts.

In a revival, people's hearts are always convicted of sin, righteousness and judgment (John 16:8). Revival never begins in the world; it begins in the Church. It starts in times of darkness, worldliness and backsliding. Revival preaching confronts sin and exposes people's hearts—that is why Satan has always attacked such preaching and labeled it "hard" or "unsophisticated." He would rather the preacher present an intellectual lecture or lead a religious parade, as that would never penetrate the hearts of the people.

Revival preaching has always contained the Law, but that has not made it legalistic. The Law also implies grace and points the way to Jesus. Then, a person who is in despair over the demands of the Law finds joy, relief and unceasing thankfulness in the grace of God. This grace, however, is not a "cheap grace." A person cannot coldly calculate on easy forgiveness, so that he continues sinning, without intending to change his life, behavior or attitudes. No! This grace streams down from heaven toward the person who despairs of his sin. He has struggled in vain to free himself. He has had a troubled conscience but could find no way out. Only the grace and revelation of Jesus can compel someone to do away with sin, follow Jesus and glorify Him. Nothing is more precious to him than this. Nothing is more vital than Jesus, God's Word, God's will and the guidance of the Spirit. He is even frightened of grieving the Holy Spirit. He is distressed over the occurrence of sin in his life and he despairs over his continuing fleshliness.

Yet he also rejoices in the deep understanding of the price that Jesus paid. He finds joy each day in the power of Jesus' blood, through which his sins are forgiven. He praises God for the wonder of becoming a new creation, and shouts out, "Hallelujah!" for the position he has been given through justification in Christ Jesus (2 Cor 5:21).

He confidently stands on the promises and flows in the gifts of grace. He is always eager to give testimony of Jesus, and he continually praises and worships God. All this is the fruit of real revival and the spirit of revival.

The Spirit of Revival
Clears the Way for True Revival

The spirit of revival, which comes as a spirit of prayer, accomplishes the following in the believer and the Church:

1. *The spirit of revival* breaks up hard ground in a person's heart, so that the Word can be sown and a harvest of fruit reaped in his life.

2. *The spirit of revival* breaks the influence of the world, sin and Satan over Christians.

3. *The spirit of revival* shows Jesus is alive. Furthermore, the Word becomes attractive and precious, and hunger for the Word increases.

4. *The spirit of revival* breaks selfishness, enhancing love and compassion for others. One looks beyond the problem areas in other Christians, and sees Jesus in them.

5. *The spirit of revival* brings fear of God and holiness.

6. *The spirit of revival* causes heathens to respect God and lose their false self-confidence.

7. *The spirit of revival* brings sensitivity to sin, sorrow over worldliness, gentleness toward others and an attentive ear for the Spirit's voice.

8. *The spirit of revival* brings a burden of prayer for sinners' salvation. There is prayer for sinners in general as well as for specific people, until they come through to salvation.

9. *The spirit of revival* encourages reconciliation and agreement between brothers.

10. *The spirit of revival* gives greater freedom in God. God is glorified in the believer's life. The flesh is kept

under so that the believer can continue to walk in victory, in the Spirit.

As the spirit of revival comes over a believer, the more joy he finds in God, but all the more are the enemy's efforts to oppose this. The devil goes to any length to keep Christians lukewarm, lethargic or confident in the flesh. He achieves this either through compromising worldliness, or rigid legalism. Many have missed revival because they immediately condemn anything which is not found in their circles, or which fails to fit into their particular theological formats.

When the spirit of revival comes over believers, doctrinal differences are transcended. God's Word is no longer used as a weapon to thump each other on the head. His Word is the source of revelation and truth, which exposes unbelief and above all, restores and sets believers free. Then the Holy Spirit can put a true burden on a receptive heart. Burdens for individuals increase, as does love for the lost and anguish over their precious souls perishing in eternity. There is also a burden for fellow believers, and for conditions in the body of Christ; sorrow for one's own weaknesses and a right compassion toward others in their weakness.

When such burdens come over believers, they are followed by a spirit of intercessory prayer. This does not relent until the issues have been prayed through, and much has been accomplished in the spirit. Out of this is birthed a genuine faith in God's promises. It is not mere intellectual consent, but a deep conviction that God really will stand for and fulfill what He has promised.

The Lord Trains Reapers for Revival

Some people have tried to force revival out of frustration—but revival comes from God. God's Spirit has been consistently directing believers to prepare, organize and train themselves so that when revival breaks out, they will know how to respond. Revival could come without preparation, trained believers and purified vessels, but it could hardly be contained, nor managed well in those circumstances.

Many revivals have been aborted because believers were not prepared to pay the price, and were poorly trained to handle the anointing and resist oppression and persecution. Often the flesh has taken over. Leadership has lacked experience, much has been wasted, and no one has nurtured the newly-saved. God does not want this. Therefore, He prepares and trains believers thoroughly so that they can tackle the problems, know how to react, stay victorious and persevere in furthering God's kingdom.

Revival is a Time of Battle and Confrontation

When revival comes, so too does a greater understanding of spiritual warfare. The Church is a home, a temple, and Christ's body, but it is also the army of God.

The whole of the Old Testament provides a graphic account of the spiritual warfare which had raged since the Fall. But Jesus disarmed the rulers and authorities of the spirit world, through His death and resurrection. He made a public display of them (Col 2:1) by His triumph over them, and it was a crushing defeat for Satan.

That victory, the triumph of the cross, was decisive, for all and for ever. *All* the princes, powers and demons of the spirit world are defeated and placed under the feet of Jesus Christ. The feet are a part of the body. That means that Satan is under our feet, under the Church, which is the body of Christ:

> "I pray that you may know... his incomparably great power for us who believe. That power is like the working of his mighty strength, which he exerted in Christ when he raised him from the dead and seated him at his right hand in the heavenly realms, far *above all* rule and authority, power and dominion, and *every title* that can be given, not only in the present age but also in the one to come. And God placed *all* things under his feet and appointed him to be head over

everything *for the church,* which is his body, the fulness of him who fills everything in every way (Eph 1:20-23).

The Church and the believer have been seated in a tremendous position of victory over the devil. *And God raised us up with Christ and seated us with him in the heavenly realms in Christ Jesus* (Eph 2:6).

This is a position of absolute triumph. The devil is attacked, defeated and disgraced, in and through Jesus at Calvary. This does *not* imply that he has been deported from this planet. A time will come when he will be banished. First, during the Millennium when he will be imprisoned in the underworld. Then in eternity, when he will be cast into the lake of burning fire. But we are not there yet!

1 Peter 5:8 says that the devil prowls about like a roaring lion, seeking someone to devour. James 4:7 says, *Resist the devil, and he will flee from you.*

In other words he is still active today, although he is defeated. If we believers do not resist him, he can hinder and harm us. There is still a war going on, no matter what some preachers say! The Church is the army of God, and Satan, with his troops, will do everything to attack, halt and defeat the Church. Therefore, times of revival are times of battle and confrontation. If you just sit and believe that revival will come like gentle rain, you have a false, romanticized picture of what revival really means.

We Fight Satan—Not People

Yes, we are seated in a high and secure position of victory *over* Satan and his spiritual powers, and we have authority in Jesus' name to exercise dominion over the enemy (Luke 10:19). Nevertheless, from this position of victory an intense battle against Satan is being waged.

For our *struggle* is not against flesh and blood, but against the rulers, against the authorities, against the powers of this dark world and against the spiritual forces of evil in the heavenly realms (Eph 6:12).

Therefore the battle continues, not against other people, but against Satan. Preachers and movements who are adamant in turning people against certain preachers, and insist on opposing their teachings and meetings, are bound to lose.

If you are in a spiritual environment where the leaders and preachers spend much of their time warning, fighting and obstructing some teaching they do not like, change your environment. Go where you can breathe fresh, spiritual air and move forwards with those who praise God out of a pure heart.

God's kingdom is a positive kingdom and His servants are positive, glad and generous servants who delight in everything God does. They are not preoccupied with destructively attacking other preachers, but busy themselves with extending God's kingdom. Though God's kingdom is a positive kingdom, it does not mean that we should never mention the enemy or what he does,

> In order that Satan might not outwit us. *For we are not unaware of his schemes* (2 Cor 2:11).

The fight is not against flesh and blood, but it is nonetheless a fight! In Luke 10:19, Jesus speaks of the *"power of the enemy,"* and that means the enemy's army. This is what Paul describes in Ephesians 6:12 when he speaks of the rulers, the forces of darkness, and the spiritual forces of wickedness in the heavenly places. There are different ranks of spiritual principalities which have different influences and areas of authority and responsibility, but their common intent is to spread the kingdom of evil here in the world. Paul also says they have limited dominion over fallen creation in the world. He uses the expression *"powers of this dark world."* Wherever the gospel has not been preached or has not penetrated, spiritual darkness has dominion. Therefore, these spiritual powers continue to reign, despite their being defeated at Calvary, and the hosts of darkness try to oppose the gospel. These hostile multitudes shoot their fiery arrows at believers, but *take up the shield of faith, with which you can extinguish all the flaming arrows of the evil one* (Eph 6:16). *He who is in you is greater than the one who is in the world* (1 John 4:4). These are promises which ensure victory!

Sent Out in Victorious Battle

We are on the winning side! We have a wonderful position of victory! Yet we are not to occupy that position and simultaneously deny the need for our armor (Eph 6), refuse to fight, and just take it easy. Paul describes the individual believer as a *good soldier of Christ* (2 Tim 2:3).

As mentioned earlier, the theme of conflict and spiritual warfare is found throughout the Bible. Any denial of this aspect would do a disservice to the body of Christ. It would only push the Church into spiritual drowsiness, giving the advantage to the enemy for an easy attack. No, this is not the time for sleeping or for decorating our walls with our spiritual missiles! We live in a time of intense spiritual preparation. We must arm and motivate ourselves.

When the Lord called us as a church, and gave us our vision, He said: "Equip My people with My word of faith. Show them their spiritual weapons, teach them how to use them, and send them out in victorious battle for Me."

Step by step, the Lord has led us in this mission, and we now send out more workers than ever throughout the world. We could never have sent them out, had we not first trained them and prepared them. But even before that, we had to realize that as believers, we are God's army.

Never let anyone rob you of being part of this victorious army. With the standard of the cross, it spreads the power of the gospel throughout the world, halts Satan's progress, and establishes Jesus' victory wherever it goes! The Church is strong, growing and aggressive. It does not retreat but advances, wielding spiritual weapons with which it pulls down strongholds (2 Cor 10:4,5), taking region after region.

Some absurdities and exaggerations may have arisen concerning spiritual warfare, but it does not mean the Church has ceased to be the army of God. Nor does it imply that we should lay down our spiritual weapons and give up. The Church should realize its identity as God's army, assume this responsibility and fight! This will bring stability, self-discipline and a sense of purpose.

Throughout Church history, the Church has been aware that, in times of revival, she has comprised a fervent, militant assembly of believers. Of course, the Church is much more than just an army. However, if out of fear of persecution, she refuses to recognize her capacity as such, she will inevitably lose her strength and her weapons. This is exactly what the enemy wants. He wants God's army to be weak, split and defenseless, for then his influence remains in the world.

We often have a romantic picture of revival, but the End-time revival will be anything but romantic. It will be world-wide and victorious. Jesus said, *"And this gospel of the kingdom will be preached in all the world as a witness to all the nations, and then the end will come"* (Matt 24:14, NKJV).

We know that we live in a time not only of revival, but of restoration. The last of the great world revivals will reap a harvest throughout the world, and then Jesus will return. That is why the Lord wants to emphasize preparation and training, since *the harvest is plentiful but the workers are few* (Matt 9:37). But perhaps we need a greater understanding of a revival atmosphere.

The Climate of the Revival Preceding Jesus' Return

Jesus describes the conditions of the times which end with the gospel having been preached all over the world, with signs and wonders, followed by His return (Matt 24). It is a time characterized by:

1. Deception (v 4,5).
2. News of wars and rumors of wars (v 6).
3. Famines and earthquakes (v 7).
4. Hate and persecution because of Jesus' name (v 9).
5. Betrayal and the falling away of many (v 10).
6. False prophets (v 11).
7. Love growing cold (v 12).
8. Increased lawlessness (v 12).

Perhaps this is not what we imagine or want to have in times of revival, but those were the conditions that Jesus foresaw at the close of the era. However, as a result of this desolate and spiritually inhospitable atmosphere, the gospel will be preached and multitudes of people will be saved. It will be a time of distinct spiritual oppression, peril and confrontation. Yet in all this, the gospel and God's power will win an overwhelming victory.

Two things are vital if we are to operate in this environment, and live in personal victory and see God's glory:

1. A strong awareness that we are all soldiers in God's army. We must know about our enemy, know our weaponry and battle strategy and know that victory is our heritage.

2. Strong, expanding, aggressive churches which have a distinct advantage in the spirit. Such churches dominate and change the spiritual atmosphere.

God knows the times we live in, and He is preparing us for the future. Through the Holy Spirit, He places emphasis on His Word, so that believers can always find nourishment. In these last days, He wants to restore all things and bring them to conclusion. The Church Age will end in victory and glory. The gospel, which has been sown throughout the centuries of the Church Age, is destined to bear a bountiful harvest before the end of this era.

The Church, the Nations and the Jews

Today, there are three main streams on which God has poured out a strong anointing. Every believer and every church which invests their energies in these will experience God moving powerfully in their lives. Often individuals, groups and churches merge into one of these currents, but God wants everyone to align themselves with all of them. These three streams flow into a specific point in the End-times, and there, Jesus will return.

1. *The first stream is the restoration of the Church.* In the Last Days, two things concerning the Church will take place.

The *first* is the falling away which the Scriptures speak of: *The Spirit clearly says that in later times some will abandon the faith and follow deceiving spirits and things taught by demons* (1 Tim 4:1).

The *second* is that the Church will be increasingly filled with God's glory. *See, darkness covers the earth and thick darkness is over the peoples, but the Lord rises upon you and his glory appears over you* (Isa 60:2).

Those grey areas in the Church will now be black and white. Hidden unbelief and sin will be exposed, and if genuine repentance does not follow, the outcome will be a falling away and a spirit of false religious harlotry. However, where God's Spirit and Word are received, his blessing, restoration and glory will flow. Then, the Church will experience tremendous growth.

2. The second stream concerns people and nations.

Darkness, hate, lawlessness, selfishness and a hardening of hearts will increase. But the spiritual drought and darkness in which many are bound will result in thousands of people rushing toward the light. They will leave the world and come into the Church of the Living God, where the gospel is preached in the power of the Holy Spirit. Revival is going to move and shake every nation before the Age of the Gentiles closes.

3. *The third stream consists of God's peculiar people, the Jews.*

When the Church Age began, the Jewish people were dispersed all over the world. But God's Word says that they will be reunited in the End-time: *Yes, I have loved you with an everlasting love; therefore with lovingkindness I have drawn you* (Jer 31:3, NKJV).

God has not forgotten His covenant and His promises to the patriarchs of Israel: *but concerning the election they are beloved for the sake of the fathers* (Rom 11:28, NKJV).

God has promised that if they are dispersed to the four corners of the earth, He will gather them together again: *For I will take you from among the nations, gather you out of all the countries, and bring you into your own land* (Ezek 36:24, NKJV). This process is accelerating as the Church Age nears its close.

In the next age—the Millennium of the Messiah's kingdom—the Jews will be reestablished and Jerusalem will become the Messiah's capital. Jerusalem will be the heart of world affairs. Today, we see Jews returning from all over the world to their country, Israel.

There is a strong resistance to this in the spirit world. The secular world and unsaved people are swayed by the spirit of anti-Semitism. They have an inherent resistance to God, His people and His country. But there are also ignorant, carnal Christians. They have accepted the false "replacement-theology" and will not acknowledge God's dealings with His special people, the Jews.

Everything Will Be Fulfilled

God's plans and purpose concerning the Church, the Gentile nations and the Jewish people, are coming to fruition as God's will is done. The Jewish people will be reunited and restored. The Gentile nations will receive a final, powerful visitation from God as the mightiest revival the world has ever seen sweeps through the earth.

The Church will come into her predestined purpose, full of power and glory. Then, Jesus will return as Head of the Church, Messiah of the Jews, Savior and Lord of all the nations. All things will be restored.

We live in a time of fulfilment. It is like the time of Joshua, when the promises of God were not only known, but fulfilled. Jesus had a powerful ministry, but this was not due to the miracles He performed, for Moses had more. Jesus' ministry was strong because He was privileged to partake in and experience the fulfilment of God's promises.

The time when the children of Israel marched over the Jordan was one of the highlights of Israel's history. Why? Because the spirit of faith that had come over Joshua and Caleb now lay over all the people. All the people stood on the same ground—the promises of God. They had the same goal, the same vision of coming into their inheritance. Everyone had found their rightful place and carried out their duties. What was the outcome? Victory!

When Joshua looked back on his life he could say, *Not one of all the Lord's good promises to the house of Israel failed; everyone was fulfilled* (Josh 21:45).

This will also happen with the Church. Everything will fall into place. Everything will be completed and there will be total victory. However, there will still be conflict, confrontation, opposition and privation, but the result will be breakthrough, victory, freedom and glory!

The Future—the Most Glorious Time

The Church has her best, yet most disastrous time ahead of her. For the half-hearted believer, the future will be depressing and more troublesome. But the future will be glorious for the person who is surrendered, loves Jesus and sets Him before all else.

The Church will arise and fulfill her destiny in God. Then, the world, whichever way it goes, will see the truth that indeed "God dwells with you" and "God is with you" (Zech 8:23).

Believers will no longer be able to lounge around in the world, sleeping in sin or indecisiveness. This is a time of decision, of self-denial, training and preparation. Believers should rise up, receive God's spoken word, His strength and power and be everything God has said. Then we will have the privilege of seeing the completion of all that God has planned.

The Church has never lived in such a time, nor been so significant! An intense battle rages around her, yet she can accomplish more than ever in the period of restoration, reformation and revival that lies ahead. The Church is approaching the most precious and glorious period in her history. Then, when the work is complete, the Lord will return.

Jesus is coming to take His Church when her mission is completed and she is prepared and adorned. He will come when everything is ready and in its place. Then, the next age will begin, stretching into eternity. In the center of it all stands Jesus, Lord of the Church, Savior of the world, King of Kings, Lord of Lords. AMEN!

Other Books by Ulf Ekman

A Life of Victory
The guidance, help and inspiration you need to put God's Word first. Fifty-four chapters, each dealing with a particular area of the believer's life. 288 pages

The Authority in the Name of Jesus
When you receive a revelation of what the name of Jesus really means, you will have boldness like never before. Booklet, 32 pages

Destroy the Works of the Devil
Jesus came to earth to destroy the works of the devil. His death on the cross struck Satan a death blow. Jesus triumphed over him and won the victory for YOU! Booklet, 32 pages

Faith that Overcomes the World
Explains how faith arises, how it becomes operational, and what makes it grow. 144 pages

Financial Freedom
A thorough, biblical study on money, riches and material possessions. 128 pages

God, the State and the Individual
God not only deals with individuals, but with nations and governments. You can change the destiny of your nation! 112 pages

God Wants to Heal Everyone
Discover the wonderful fact that God's will is to heal everyone—including you.
Booklet, 32 pages

The Jews—People of the Future
Clarifies basic truths about the people and the land.
Historical facts and Biblical prophecies combine to reveal
the fulfillment of God's End-time Plan. 160 pages

The Power in the New Creation
A new dimension of victorious living awaits you. The Lord
is with you, Mighty Warrior!
Booklet, 32 pages

The Prophetic Ministry
*"Provides essential guideposts for the operation of the
prophetic ministry today."* From the Foreword by Demos
Shakarian. 224 pages

Available from your local Christian bookstore, or order
direct from the publisher:

Word of Life Publications
GPO Box 2375, Brisbane, Qld 4001, Australia
Box 641, Marine Parade, Singapore 9144
Box 17, S-751 03 Uppsala, Sweden
Box 70, Oxted, Surrey, RH8 0YS, United Kingdom
Box 46108, Minneapolis, MN 55446, USA